CLOTHES**MINDED**
BY CHRISTINE MORRISON

FASHIONABLE ESSAYS
ABOUT FINDING YOURSELF

Advance Praise for Clothes Minded: Fashionable Essays About Finding Yourself

Clothes Minded captures the transformative power of the clothes we wear and the stories they hold. Sharp, stylish and unexpectedly heartfelt, this collection of personal essays had me reliving my own fashion eras and the style reinventions that shaped my life and career. It's a fashion biography that resonates far beyond the closet.

— Lori Singer, President Parlux Fragrances

CLOTHES MINDED

Fashionable Essays About Finding Yourself

CHRISTINE MORRISON

Elevate Press

Disclaimer

This book is a memoir. It reflects the author's present recollections of experiences over time. Some names and characteristics have been changed to protect the privacy of individuals, some events have been compressed and some dialogue has been recreated.

For James, Cameron and MacEwen.
You are my everything.

Contents

Prologue

FASHION. With a capital F.

IT'S NOT FRIVOLOUS. It's not exclusive. You shouldn't be required to pronounce Ann Demeulemeester ("de-mule-eh-meester"), tap into your 401(k) or buy coveted Gucci knee-high socks to understand that what we wear matters. Choosing a look is never just about fabric—it's a decision that telegraphs who we are and who we aspire to become. The clothes in my tightly edited closet reflect both my reality and my ambitions every day. My choices are deliberate. As Miuccia Prada once said, "What you wear is how you present yourself to the world, especially today, when human contacts are so quick. Fashion is instant language." And, yes, it speaks louder than words.

FASHION, for me, has always been more than silhouettes and trends. It's memory, identity, rebellion, armor—and at times, escape. My ever-evolving wardrobe mirrors my growth, shapes my voice, and helps me reclaim parts of myself. I've never admired style from afar. I built a career within it. I worked across several major beauty brands, including Olay, Jergens and John Frieda, helping craft identities, tell brand stories and forge emotional connections with consumers. In those roles—behind the scenes, yet at the center of brand development—I discovered how deeply style, image, and self-perception are intertwined. Later, as vice president of marketing at Calvin Klein, I saw firsthand what I always suspected: fashion is far from frivolous. It's a profound expression of who we are.

OVER TIME, I've come to appreciate the symbiotic relationship between personal growth and style evolution. Fashion is a metaphor, a tangible expression of the intangible: the moments of doubt, triumph and transformation that define us. Each piece of clothing we choose carries a story, an emotion, a memory stitched into its seams or soles.

THIS COLLECTION of essays is a reflection of that journey. Some are embroidered with nostalgia, others are hemmed in hard lessons. But each one is grounded in a simple truth: fashion is a language—and for me, it's always been fluent though sometimes hard to master. There's a line Andy Barnard said in *The Office* that stays with me: "I wish there was a way to know you're in the good old days before you've actually left them." It's not just sentimentality; it's the flicker of recognition sparked by an old outfit or dated hair. These choices contributed to our growth, development and self-discovery. (Even if we didn't fully appreciate the effect at the time.) This collection is my way of honoring those moments—*the good old days*—even when I didn't initially realize their value.

Whether you're here for the behind-the-scenes industry stories, cultural commentary or a reminder that personal style is a powerful form of self-expression, welcome. These observations and recollections invite you to view fashion as more than the clothes you slip on each morning. With intention, they become the identity you step into every day. Because spoiler alert: this book isn't just about me. It's about all of us. We've all been shaped by what we've worn.

THE CHAPTERS unfold decade by decade, each threaded with flashbacks through the lens of my fashion choices: Ann Taylor suits, agnès b shoes, Theory pencil skirts, whimsical Cynthia Rowley pants and scandalously low-rise Seven jeans. But always, I circle back to my mainstay: crisp white button-down shirts, my personal superhero cape, which help me feel capable and in control during life crises, from an epilepsy diagnosis in my thirties to a later miscarriage. These days, as I head to carpool in my pared-down uniform (still *a lot* of J.Crew), I no longer need sartorial camouflage. I've become the woman I never expected to be—and that, in itself, is a wondrous triumph.

I'VE LONG ADMIRED the unique personal style of so many women. Curious how they found their fashion ease, I asked a handful—designers, stylists and industry trailblazers—to share their fashion motivations and tips. Their voices come together as the Epilogue, aptly titled "Famous Last Words." Among them are stylist Sarah Clary, KULE founder Nikki Kule, FRĒDA SALVADOR co-founder Megan Papay, Vintner's Daughter founder April Gargiulo and Dorsey founder Meg Strachan.

These thoughtful women share more than personal memories. They offer style philosophies and actionable takeaways. Consider these tips a little style cheat sheet—some offer a go-to piece; others, a mindset shift. Think of these fashion monologues as needed reminders that style can still spark joy, even on a dreary Monday, and more importantly, as we age.

Their contributions and my narrative are not just style stories. They are human tales, told through clothes, beauty, memory and meaning. Some of my chapters are soft recollections. Others unspool the harder truths. But they all share one underlying belief: what we wear is never just about appearances. It's one of the most accessible, democratic and intimate ways we communicate our true selves.

SO, wherever you are in your relationship with fashion—whether you're navigating a new chapter in your career, rediscovering your personal style after years of putting others first or simply showing up bleary-eyed for your morning coffee—I hope these pages resonate. And reflect, somewhere along the way, your own story, too.

I wrote this book to remember. To trace how we got here. To hold space for the versions of ourselves we've outgrown and the iterations we've yet to meet. Because the truth is, as we age, we don't need the good old days to define us. Fashion, after all, is not just about the clothes we wear; it's about the courage to embrace who we are right now—and the changes that guide us forward.

The Nineties

ONE

French Girls Don't Wear Ann Taylor

THESE DAYS, you can't swing a belted trench coat without hitting an editor, influencer or model exhorting ways to be effortlessly chic like a "French girl." The nearly seven million #frenchgirl Instagram posts are hardly a trend. There are new imported beauty brands like Violette FR and La Bouche Rouge pushing insouciant looks, though you must credit Chanel for literally naming a nude gloss "Insouciance." You also see French pharmacy skincare finds like La Roche-Posay and Vichy (only the European versions brought back in a suitcase, s'il vous plaît) topping editorial lists and the rise of gamine fashion labels like Sézane, Carel and Maje. Mon Dieu, we're living in Breton-striped madness. You must be chic and elegant yet effortless; appear tousled, while being buttoned up. Even Jane Birkin, who festooned her namesake Birkin with stickers and Greek worry beads, would agree we have taken this aesthete too far.

As a freshly minted journalism alumna transplanted to Chicago in the early '90s, I knew about as much about French New Wave cinema and Hermès as I did true style. High school French notwithstanding, I was a cheerleading, strait-laced all-American girl who wore shiny gloss in pink instead of femme-fatale red. I grew up in the heartbeat of prep, Baltimore, wearing

Izod Lacoste alligator polos and navy Tretorns. I idolized stat-uesque waspy beauties like Christie Brinkley and Niki Taylor while studying every page of *Seventeen Magazine*. Despite some growth in my periodical preferences—I subscribed to and pored over *Vogue, Mademoiselle* and *Glamour* cover to cover in college —my post-collegiate lifestyle was equally far from chic and my wardrobe as enviable as my career. Meaning, no one was jealous of me. I was the Andy Sachs of my ad agency as I helmed the recep-tion desk, a U-shaped, driftwood brown work surface the size of a family-style dining table, equipped with a blinking phone, "while you were out" message pads, and a stack of blue Bic pens. I told myself I was settling in, but really, I was just settling. College comfort and checking account minimums trumped fashion, so my Ann Taylor graduation suit and some, often polyester blend, separates were my attempt at polished office looks.

The fashion elite's French girl aesthetic was not just foreign to me, but also a world away from my closet of stiff upper-lip staples like pressed shirts and constrained cable knit sweaters. My long blonde wavy hair, however, reeked of haute bohemia. It gave me a "just rolled out bed" allure that aligned with carefree, cool Parisian girls and their undone mascot, Brigitte Bardot. I loved that Bardot, who originated the title "sex kitten," was more than just a beautiful face and bombshell body. She symbolized the sexual revolution, a movement that freed women to celebrate being single rather than following the traditional path of virginity until marriage.

In my twenties, having left my college beau behind on campus, my plan was to be liberated and louche. My effortless hair complied with my new carefree identity and called for just that: minimal effort. Proficient in part-time and weekend jobs, I kept my locks low maintenance as a necessity as much as a style. To appear more well-kempt in the office, I'd pull my mane back in a knot with a neutral scrunchie. Scrunchies were my Cartier LOVE bracelet. When not looped around my locks, I welded one to my wrist as a sign of commitment to my longest relationship: my hair.

Banana clips, ubiquitous in their plastic glory, offended me. They screamed flag football, which I didn't play despite it being *the* thing to do to meet people in Lincoln Park, my picturesque yuppie neighborhood. I let my hair down, while waiting tables every weekend at the corner bar Grants or folding candy-color sweaters at J.Crew when the holidays hit. These jobs constituted my social life and financed my lifestyle, which consisted of little more than hanging out with friends in neighborhood bars and in crowded apartments with too many roommates for my taste. We'd spend weekend afternoons window shopping Lincoln Park boutiques, with me always dreaming about my next purchase, riding bikes along the lakefront and laughing. It's all I could afford to do. My receptionist salary crested just above the federal poverty level (even the government recognized I needed more money), but I refused to look the part of an entry-level cliché.

While I fielded calls for a living, I had the privilege of watching the sly and sometimes salacious interactions of everyone passing through the ad agency. I also overheard juicy gossip because everyone ignores the receptionist. But rumors of affairs and calls from disgruntled spouses didn't interest me. I had ambition and busied myself with figuring out who I needed to know to move up—and out—of my pre-entry level role. I gravitated toward creatives; I admired the art directors, photographers and stylists who lounged around the lobby as much for their work as their ease with style. One of my favorite photography reps worked for Victor Skrebneski, the legendary fashion photographer who'd discovered Cindy Crawford and helmed Estée Lauder campaigns since the early sixties. He shot the iconic "Estée Lauder Woman" campaign. Another rep, a chatty older French gentleman named Jacques, wore cravats unironically and expressed interest in me beyond my ability to make his appointments start on time. Once, as I was thumbing through *Mademoiselle*, he turned the cover and said, "Mademoiselle. How fitting." I felt seen. People didn't often talk to me, the receptionist. They talked *at* me. But somehow Jacques didn't miss me.

There was little dignity to my job. They forced me to take breaks from the front desk, as if I worked a grueling shift at a factory. One afternoon, I intersected with Jacques in the elevator bank. He looked me over, more with pity than lust. I could practically read his mind, as he discerned my style more "campus mixer" than "creative up-and-comer."

"Want to check out Neiman Marcus with me, Mademoiselle?" he asked with his architectural eyebrows raised.

Our agency, centrally located on North Michigan Avenue and perched seven stories above Neiman Marcus, was the perfect place to daydream about fashion and beauty. Off the printed page. I'd ridden the escalators woven through the stunning store but never ventured into the elegant departments boasting large logoed hangers of Prada, Gucci and Chanel. Receptionists can't pay retail. Even Neiman's notorious Last Call sale prices were too steep. I already ate enough ramen.

That day, Jacques took me by the elbow as we descended the escalators to the beauty department on the first floor, where glass counters reflected sunlight, and women in fitted skirt suits and heels flitted around like honeybees. It smelled like Chanel No. 5 wafted from the vents. Or maybe it was just Jacques' French pheromones? Flashbacks of visiting Hutzler's, the "grande dame of Baltimore department stores" in its heyday, with my grandmother Cordelia came back to me in that moment. We'd have afternoon tea like ladies who lunch before stopping by the makeup counter for her only luxury purchases: a sickly sweet, bourbon-colored perfume called Youth Dew and a bold red Estée Lauder lipstick. She let me don her emerald and diamond ring, with several Band-Aids at the base to secure the fit, and eagerly skip through the store to touch *everything*. These stylish adventures ended abruptly before I turned nine when she passed. The ring was buried in a cousin's jewelry box following the funeral. I've been gun-shy about falling for accessories ever since. They are often so personal. Even at age eight, I knew they were small reminders of people we love and moments we'd cherish. When she passed, I felt fragile without my grand-mother's ring. I've never felt ready to face that kind of heart-break again.

As if he were going to get a cut on the sale, Jacques swiftly led me to the first beauty counter to explore Origins, a brand that launched the previous year in 1990. Origins, while created by Estée Lauder's eldest son, Leonard, was the first department store skincare to use natural ingredients, he explained. Don't ask me why this Parisian dandy knew about organic serums. I spotted the bland recycled packaging with its tree logo and assumed it catered to hippie environmentalists, not someone like me who longed to be beautiful and more sophisticated. I zoned out as the sales-woman droned on about indigenous healing, environmentally friendly policies and regimens. But I happily snapped to attention when she handed me a color coordinated cleanser, toner and mineral-enriched moisturizer.

She gently ran her hands over my face and full eyebrows—the same arches I would pluck to wispy crescent moons a few years later to bow to a trend—and said something about my youthful skin. Yes, my skin reeked of youth. Not in a soft, well-hydrated sense, but rather in a "I drank beer and devoured pizza at 2 a.m." way. We both knew I neglected my outer beauty. She slyly suggested an active charcoal mask and "Peace of Mind" aromatherapy cream that would do wonders for my skin, while she simultaneously rang the products up. And beautify my soul, she added, sounding like a sidewalk soothsayer. I doubted her. I could not imagine how skincare could profoundly change my life. I handed over my credit card, just in case. I wanted to look, and let's be honest, *feel* a little pretty. My confidence was running on empty, right alongside my checking account. But beauty (over)promised a quick fix and a morale boost, and I was willing to believe it. Unlike fashion, it was at least within reach. Jacques smiled knowingly, then whispered to me in his heavy Gallic drawl, "Effortless beauty."

Careful not to go over on my phone minutes that night, I

succinctly told my mother about the excursion. "What are his intentions?" she probed, ever protective.

"I'm not exactly his type, Mom," I retorted. "And I nearly gave him a heart attack when I told him my current regimen includes Neutrogena and Sea Breeze. This was a charity mission."

Within days, I'd embraced my new skincare routine. The trio of glass containers stood prominently displayed on my dresser like works of art. I never fell asleep without taking a few minutes to knead the peppermint, basil and eucalyptus essential oils blended in the "Peace of Mind" treatment on my temples and neck. It was unaware self-care. It worked, too. I felt more put together, even when I used the excess product on my palms to tame my wild hair. It was lovely but not effortless. Beauty, even in my small ritual, required consistency for efficacy.

Weeks later, I was Eliza Doolittle again. Jacques, a.k.a my determined Henry Higgins, wanted to introduce me to agnès b., the timeless French brand known for being chic yet casual. The label's bestseller was, and still is, a cardigan with snap buttons. Once an editor at *Elle* magazine, the founder Agnes Trouble gleaned inspiration from flea market finds and designed for women to express their individual personality. I was just discovering myself, Jacques said to me, so it was a great place to start identifying a style. I could not argue that I already had a look with my suave mentor. That day, my style consisted of Gap khakis and a pressed button-down. Nondescript fashion at its finest. I knew I wanted more for myself. I longed for clothes that reflected my essence. Jacques intuited my desire. "The French archetype is just the best, non?" he asked.

Oui, but I had never entered the austere agnès b. store on Oak Street, lined with all the best luxury brands in Chicago, out of fear of the unknown. The price tags terrified me even more. But after a lunch hour of perusing, trying on clothes and discussing fashion —as if I were allowed to be part of the conversation—I sashayed out with a pair of black block-heeled loafers with a large white buckle on top. They mimicked a Chanel shoe but allowed me to still pay rent. They also elevated my French girl aesthetic, clearly Jacques' intent given his adoration for his motherland. But as he escorted me back to the office, I sensed he was equally delighted to have shown me a way to dress that stretched my imagination while still aligning with my minimalist DNA.

I wore those agnès b. loafers for twenty years. The ultimate in cost per wear. They carried me into my career building renowned beauty brands (none were French) and then working in-house for the (American) maestro of minimalism, Calvin Klein. They were re-soled until they fell apart, replaced by the ultimate French girl shoe: ballet flats. I'd love to say Jacques came to mind when I bought my first pair of black Repetto ballet flats, but it was Kate Moss. She wore them repetitively, with everything from skinny jeans to leather miniskirts to Capri pants. Kate made ballet flats edgy and versatile—and spurred my enduring love for the shoe.

Fashion exec energy at age 10; I'm far left with popped collar.

I've often wished I could reunite with Jacques to say in a perfect accent, "merci beaucoup." I will never know what drew him to become my style sherpa. Months after our shopping sprees, I got a new job—the kind that actually makes it onto the resume—in another advertising agency. And with it came greater purchasing power. My Ann Taylor garb vanished like Jacques as I learned how to incorporate agnès b. and other simple (less flammable) fashion into my wardrobe. But I never forgot those excursions, where dressing room three-way mirrors became my passport; they were as close as I'd get to France for the foreseeable future. My time with Jacques emboldened me. I was no longer a timid tourist window shopping in my own city. I wish Jacques could trace my sartorial journey that, thanks to his guidance, led me to become a better dressed young women with incredibly hydrated skin. But more importantly, his direction helped me deeply understand how to shop for pieces that echoed and even enhanced my true self. Despite rebuffing my entry-level attire, he was no label snob. He gently steered me to styles that reflected not only who I was, but also who I wanted to become. "You have big dreams. Shouldn't your wardrobe show that?" he once asked. Jacques didn't urge me to "dress for the job you want." That was too limiting. He encouraged me to create a wardrobe for the life I was pioneering.

As the French girl aesthetic surpassed sartorial inspiration, escalating to a cultural obsession, fashion and beauty mavens—and the last of the remaining fashion magazines—began calling its bluff. "It's a fantasy!" headlines cried. "A mythology!" Influencers on TikTok shrieked. I agree. There are not enough striped shirts, trench coats, red lipsticks or cigarettes to make this feminine ideal, the trope of the perennially chic Parisian, a reality. It's not attainable. Even Elizabeth Hawes, the legendary fashion designer and author of the 1938 indictment of the business of style *Fashion is Spinach* once declared, "There is no word in English for chic. Why should there be? Everything chic is by legend French." She knew we'd get to this point. The French girl aesthetic is overhyped and as Hawes foretold: "Chic is a combination of style and fashion. To be really chic, a woman must have a positive style, a positive way of living and acting and looking which is her own."

When Barneys opened in Chicago years later, across from

agnès b. naturally, I was prepared. I'd been perusing Henri Bendel since concluding Jacques' tutorials. Rarely did I buy anything, but I frequently explored indie beauty brands they exclusively carried like MAC and their iconic brown-and-white striped toiletries bags. At Barneys, I dove curtain bangs first (I was not above the French girl fringe) into NARS beauty and Barneys private label, designed by Behnaz Sarafpour. Both offered a *je ne sais quoi* spirit I knew would both make Jacques proud and put me at ease. A tall order for a relatively insecure twenty-five-year-old. I wore the line's chic, functional and well-made crewneck cashmere sweaters, dresses and miniskirts paired with camo-colored nail lacquer (aptly coined "Mash") on repeat; my look felt cool but uncomplicated and gave me space to unearth my individual aesthetic.

Regardless of my early French influence, I ultimately found nothing is truly carefree and effortless. It all takes work. Especially as we age. Brigitte Bardot, at ninety, doesn't fight growing older, leaning into her wiry gray hair with the same ease and confidence that made her an icon. That's the real French girl aesthetic—not youth but embracing what you have. While the French girl facade may appear enviable, it's more of a concept, a paper dolls approach to fashion and beauty. And there are no more mademoiselles. *Mademoiselle* magazine folded in 2001 and in the following decade, the French government banned the youthful term as lobbying women's groups deigned it "sexist."

But I found my own version of French girl appeal, which is exactly what Jacques intended. I realized that my wind-blown, undone hair did not need a vintage Hermes scarf to appear carefree. My lips, rich with Chapstick rather than rouge lipstick, did not make me any less chic. I began to feel good about myself as I stepped into my own. I may have been as far from being an "It girl" with a French aesthetic as landing a coveted job at *Vogue*, but I was just beginning to blossom. Effortlessly.

TWO

Saturday Mornings with Elsa Klensch

IT WAS the '90s and Supermodels reigned supreme. Coined The Trinity—Naomi, Christy, Linda—then The Big Five, with Cindy and Claudia added to the mix, and then eventually The Big Six to make room for Kate Moss, they wouldn't get out of bed for less than $10,000. When industry domination wasn't enough for these leggy clothes horses, the one-named wonders began to squabble publicly over the "Original Supermodels" title. They were the faces of a generation; even *Time* magazine declared supermodels more glamorous than movie stars. Bombshell alert: I wasn't one of them.

But I did worship style. Every Saturday morning, I sat on the faded hardwood floor of my Chicago apartment watching CNN's *Style with Elsa Klensch* taking notes as if there'd be a quiz, post-show. As a born perfectionist with a fashion fixation since in utero, it's no coincidence that my blood type is A+. There's no doubt I would have aced the test; what I was failing in was glamour. While the supermodels I adored wouldn't budge without their bankroll, my ancient television required pliers to change channels and its antennae wore an aluminum foil headdress. I was broke. I worked in advertising, where the culture was more recreation than compensation. The more fun the agency, the less you were paid.

What I lacked in designer garb, however, I made up for in grooming, ironed clothes and polished shoes. I was the only girl I knew with starched Gap khakis. I lived in Biore Pore Strips. I didn't branch out from my inexpensive mainstays: uninspiring trousers and blazers from The Gap and Banana Republic. These bland brands suited my account executive agency job until sales for Nirvana's *Nevermind* album escalated. When grunge took a chokehold on style, I added thrift store Levi's into the mix. The denim on heavy rotation was slightly cropped and had a remarkable imprinted circle on the back right pocket, thanks to the previous owner's fierce Skoal habit. I also succumbed to floral dresses from Anthropologie—which, at the time, felt more refined than Urban Outfitters—and wore "Paramount," the ubiquitous dark lipstick from MAC Cosmetics. No lip liner, thanks. But it was the lace-up Doc Marten boots that I most adored. Before long, I was wearing them with wide-leg trousers and under bridesmaid gowns; fitting, as I was in my late twenties and everyone was getting married. Not me. I was committed to figuring out what I wanted to be when I grew up. When the era of grunge ended, I was honestly relieved. Beyond slovenly, it was not a good look on my just over five-foot frame. Doc Martens, however, became a forever shoe— and still sit patinaed in my closet today.

Long before there was Queen Elsa of Arendelle, my generation's Elsa garnered a devoted following, and I was one of her unwavering subjects. Every weekend on CNN, her in-depth profiles of design legends, as well as up-and-comers like Todd Oldham, Patrick Robinson and Helmut Lang, were delivered from on-high, all in a darling, yet raspy, Australian accent. Having worked at *Vogue* and *Harper's Bazaar*, Elsa Klensch sported fashion editor hair: the trademark glossy bob and bangs that would go on to become synonymous with the world's most (in)famous Editor-In-Chief, Anna Wintour. Despite my fashion aspirations, I planned to preserve my Sarah Jessica Parker, then Robert Downey Jr.'s girlfriend, long curly hair.

I was front and center from the start of each *Style* episode, regardless of what time I went to sleep on Friday night. I hated to miss the runway montages blended with classical music that kicked off each half hour of fantasy Elsa streamed into my living room. Her show propelled me to imagine a life in New York City, working in fashion. She was considered the grand dame who invented fashion television, whereas I, at age twenty-eight, had only succeeded in creating a system for keeping ratty college T-shirts in order of date received— Spring Fling 1989 never sat in its neat, Gap-style folded stack above 1990's "Après Ski" Winter Formal.

Decades before I could be found lovingly piling my T-shirts in chronological order, I had a penchant for clothing design. My mother claims my fascination was obsessive as a kid growing up in Baltimore. By age seven, I loved getting dressed in the morning and often changed outfits by midday on weekends. There was a jumper that had to be worn for school pictures—two years in a row. To make it pop the second time around, I paired it with a new fire engine red pussy bow blouse. I even cuffed my denim pants for several seasons. My clothes were known as "my wardrobe" before I really knew what that meant. (I'd heard an older friend of my mother's use the word and thought it sounded sophisticated.) I wore orange trousers habitually one summer. I was a walking Clementine, my citrus legs snugly fitted in high waters à la Thom Browne's designs decades later. A swim team friend sang, "and a bright orange pair of pants" (from Billy Joel's 1980 hit "It's Still Rock and Roll to Me") each time she glanced my way.

It was important for me to stand out from the Garanimals crowd. *The Official Preppy Handbook* was my Bible when it was released in 1980, but I strove to distinguish myself from the

Middle School Muffys, as I found head-to-toe pink and green gauche. I longed for button-downs in neutral tones, Add-a-Bead necklaces and a Bermuda bag without the whimsical Nantucket motifs like spouting whales or Technicolor coral. My favorite store was called "Daddy's Money." Talk about a patriarchal play. But this shop was so high-priced that I could never afford a purchase, no matter how many hours of babysitting I accrued— or how much I begged my father. While walking though, I would trail my fingers over the Deans of Scotland sweaters, imagining what it might feel like to wear the Fair Isle wool. Despite my commitment to prep and popping my collars, a more monochromatic color scheme spoke to me—even as a twelve-year old. I had never heard the word "minimalism," but I believed it was my innate style. That doesn't mean I snubbed the pastel braided barrettes my friends made and sold. I was charitable. But more importantly, as a suburban tween, I desperately wanted to fit in. I wanted to express my identity through what I wore, but not at the risk of being an outcast.

Beverly Cleary in hand, red bow on point.

GIVEN MY CHILDHOOD FASCINATION, I was born to watch Elsa weekly. Her Saturday morning runway coverage was the ultimate escape for me. Especially when designers like Ralph Lauren and Calvin Klein created empires not based on fabric, but on dreams. I didn't need to live in Ralph's oceanfront Montauk home to feel less trapped by my measly 500-square-foot apartment, riddled with a dorm size, under-the-counter refrigerator, but just seeing it—the pristine white compound previously owned by John Lennon and Yoko Ono—was enough to thrust me into dreaming of a new life. I knew I had a calling but was still watching ample *Oprah* to glean enough courage to take a leap. She swore her inner voice, and subsequently following her intuition, led to success. "Every day, your life is speaking to you, telling you *exactly* where you should be going. Are you listening?" Oprah would ask on my VCR recordings. Alas, my life spoke in a faint whisper. My intuition had been trained from an early age to use an indoor voice.

I learned through Elsa that designers also see the runway as an escape, an outlet to reveal their art. While today runways are so often "see now, buy now," designers used to parade unwearable, architectural pieces down the catwalk; while they were rarely produced, there was no better way to showcase their talent. In the best of circumstances, these displays of creativity would morph into something that can actually go on a rack at Macy's. Or be worn by a Kardashian. Because brands need sales and good press to survive.

Elsa understood the delicate balance of art and commerce. She treated designers with the respect they deserved. I can't imagine what she would have made of the modern-day spectacle of fashion. CNN canceled her show in 2001, so she couldn't gasp at the awkward debacle of "front row casting," a more recent ploy that makes the A-list audience more important than the fashion itself. And don't even get me started on celebs who sat courtside at couture shows but couldn't be bothered to take off baseball hats or even don underwear. It was a low chapter in fashion history.

On most Saturdays during the '90s, I sat rapt on the sofa in my Gap pajama bottoms and a white men's shirt with rolled cuffs and popped collar, a look I stole from Carolina Herrera. Yes, I dressed to be front row ready. I could never afford Herrera's namesake luxury brand, but I admired her timeless, sophisticated designs—crafted to make women feel confident, rather than sexy or on display. The fact that she launched her fashion career at forty gave me, another late bloomer, hope. In my mind, I still had time: Time to find myself. Time to make my dreams reality. The ever-elegant Herrera sent ballgowns and daytime dresses down the runway, but she always relied on a uniform of a crisp white shirt with a popped collar. *That*, I could afford. "I love white shirts because they feel like a security blanket," Herrera once said. "Whatever you want to be, the white shirt becomes."

One day, while I was engrossed in Elsa's take on Ralph Lauren's 1997 Fall runway show that opened with a model in a white deep cut men's shirt before leading into peasant looks, my boyfriend B wandered into my apartment. We met in our advertising agency jobs. B, an art director, knew more about making Claymation movies than he did about navigating relationships, but he was adorable, and made me laugh. It was just what I needed. With one shoe (my bulky Doc Martens) in my twenties and the other (a sleek Steve Madden kitten heel) tiptoeing into my thirties, I was at an existential standstill. It was bad enough that I didn't feel like an adult. Even worse, I had yet to make any significant strides toward my future. This fun, lighthearted fling with B helped derail the mounting anxiety I felt about my next steps.

After a quick peck, so as not to disturb my concentration, B's cheek grazed my starched collar as he peeked into my notebook. I proudly showcased my Helvetica-like handwriting meticulously lining the blank pages. He found my OCD charming; it was still early in the relationship. "Do you iron those shirts yourself?" he once asked, realizing how often I wore a white men's shirt. I could only smile. I wasn't ready to let on how much joy ironing brought me, how cathartic it felt to have the rising steam hit my face. Or that I went out of my way to get lavender-scented spray starch. But that day, instead of asking questions about Elsa's interview or finding my fashion research habit charming, he looked at my notes, looked at me, then said, "You don't think *you're* going to be a model, do you?"

Silence compressed the already diminutive living room. Even Elsa's oration about Lauren's genius muted. Perpetually loquacious me was rendered speechless. But this was the opposite of a mic drop. There was no triumph here. We were supposed to be in the honeymoon phase of dating, having been together a few short months. Isn't that when you adore everything about one another? You know, before someone quits politely putting the toilet seat down or refilling the ice trays. We were creative kindred spirits, I thought, finding each other's habits—my writing and his drawing —admirable and sweet. Just the weekend prior, we'd bicycled north of the city limits to spend hours lying on Northwestern University campus' plush green lawn. While savoring each other's presence, discussing books, movies, and talking ad nauseam about ad campaigns from the world-renowned advertising agency where we met, I felt a shift. Amongst the spread of Snapples and soggy tuna fish sandwiches, I thought I could talk to him about anything. We were more than just spending time with each other; we were forging a future together. But suddenly, for the first time, I felt judged—and clearly misunderstood. Of course, I didn't have aspirations to rival Cindy or Naomi. I mean, I stood just over five feet tall on the most positive of posture days. Plus, I'd devoured the past 144 issues of *Glamour, W* and *Vogue*. Thank to those magazines, I knew more than fifty ways to tie a scarf and the true purpose of skin care toner. More importantly, I had a clear take-away: I was not model material. Not even strip-mall J.C. Penney winter coat model material. Being blessed—or cursed, depending on which angle I was being photographed—with Barbra Streisand's nose didn't help matters. In fact, I was already one and a half rhinoplasties in and seeking out a new surgeon. I was cute, at best. "I am many things," I thought to myself. "But a wannabe model is not one of them." Mostly, I was floored by his crassness.

While I silently seethed, B plopped onto the floor and began flipping through the thin January issues of *Vogue*, *Mademoiselle* and *Glamour* magazines. There had to be an article in one of those about dating an asshole boyfriend, but it was too late for him. He probably wouldn't have taken the hint anyway. With my hand shaking in frustration, I clutched the pliers to turn off the TV before taking a deep breath. I had watched enough *Oprah*— and could credit a phenomenal, headstrong mother who raised me well—to know that to be loved, you must be known. Fully. I may have been immature, but I was savvy enough to know that revealing your true self is the only way to real intimacy. In that moment, I realized that B was just an affair, not a love affair. He didn't question my ambition, but he didn't share it either. And I was starting to understand that was not going to be enough for me. This wasn't about modeling clothes. It was about being naked. I didn't know if my dreams would ever come true, but I believed I deserved the chance to find out—and someone beside me who believed that too.

Up until then, B had been a lot like a wardrobe staple I donned daily: the slip dress. They were both easygoing, forgiving of flaws, and worked well with my lifestyle. It wasn't Elsa's 1990 interview with a young Anna Wintour, severely cropped bob in place but not yet hiding behind her signature saucer-sized sunglasses, that sold me on the slip dress. Wintour's comment, "The whole concept of innerwear as outwear is revolutionizing" echoed the sentiment of every designer of that era. I may have admired the British editrix, but my utter infatuation was for then Calvin Klein publicist Carolyn Bessette Kennedy, who—along with Kate Moss—was one of those most iconic slip dress advocates of the era. Carolyn proved the garment could be more prude than provocative, a clean slate to showcase her individuality as she wore it pared back and with understated accessories like her "power headband." In the end, the slip dress wasn't just her uniform, but, in part, her legacy. As *CBK: Carolyn Bessette Kennedy: A Life in Fashion* author Sunita Kumar Nair put it, "She always wore slip dresses but now she chose to wear [one] for her wedding dress." Former CFDA executive director Fern Mallis agreed: In wearing the Narcisco Rodriguez slip dress, "She literally changed the bridal industry."

Likewise, I felt my knee-length black bias-cut slip dresses were a canvas for my budding personality, worn everywhere and with everything neutral, from cardigans and pullovers to men's shirts tied at the waist and blazers. Unlike Carolyn, I owned a limited amount of apparel, had no expendable income and often waitressed on weekends in the same clothes I wore to work at the ad agency. She may have been of great interest to the public and paparazzi, thanks in part to her incredible style, but I was the best-dressed bar waitress in Lincoln Park at the time.

With the supermodel inquisition still dangling in the air between us, B lost most of his luster. He had no idea how much his words bruised me. And as I sat staring at the chipped paint on my ceiling's crown molding, I knew I had a choice. I could learn from this moment—which was not just humiliating but also illuminating—and break up with him to find a like-minded partner, not just a coworker-turned-companion. Or I could speak up and try to move the relationship forward with honesty. Tugging at my cuffs, I knew that I was, in part, to blame. After all, I had not shared enough of my true self. And I knew I had big dreams, maybe even delusional ones, that did not include him. Like the obvious cracks appearing through the spackled white walls of my Old Town apartment, I could now see this relationship for what it was: a fun runway trend of the time like bucket hats or bicycle shorts. I may not have watched all of the 40,000 fashion shows Elsa covered, but I certainly listened and learned when she said, "Real luxury is beauty and love." The inevitable breakup happened one week later, on the day after Halloween. Hey, he was a fantastic art director after all, and I wanted a spectacular pumpkin carving.

In the end, I learned something essential: I could compromise on comfort. I could play with styles and silhouettes. But I wasn't willing to tailor my needs to fit someone else's idea of a future. Fashion gave me space to grow—to evolve, to shape who I was and to imagine who I could become. Love should, too.

THREE

Love Lessons from Trina Turk

IN THE LATE '90S, beauty brands were (skin) deep in the business of empowerment. They stopped selling lipstick and started selling confidence. Commercials became affirmations; marketing campaigns promised not just transformation, but self-actualization. Maslow's hierarchy of needs may have been fifty years old, but women were finally making themselves—and their girl power—the priority. In this landscape, the phrase *Make yourself happy* more than tripled in Google Book's American database between 1990 and 2008. Equally liberating mantras like *Don't need anyone* (which had never previously registered), *Never compromise*, and *I love me* were also on the rise. A self-esteem craze had taken over the country, leaving participation trophies in its wake.

I was in the throes of college, at The University of North Carolina at Chapel Hill, when feeling good about yourself first became a national pastime. Self-care had yet to hit the zeitgeist and there was zero prescience it would escalate to today's almost $7 trillion global industry. With my BA in Journalism and loads of professor-induced self-esteem, however, I felt empowered to leave my college sweetheart to embark on my own to Chicago the minute I shed my polyester graduation gown. It was the *Murphy*

Brown decade after all, and L'Oréal kept telling me, "I'm worth it." Women were free to aspire wildly, be anything or anyone they desired. My desire? Work in one of Chicago's premier advertising agencies. Maybe even McCann Erickson, where L'Oréal's infamous tagline originated. And I wanted to go it alone.

Unlike the women who fought for rights before me (thanks, Gloria Steinem!), I didn't need to burn a bra to gain equality. I was surfing the "third wave of feminism" and loving the strides being made with pregnancy medical leave, "Take Our Daughters to Work" day, and newfound political power. Sure, Dianne Feinstein of California and Janet Reno as First Attorney General made for impressive role models, but the thrill was also to be found right in my new backyard witnessing Carol Moseley Braun of Illinois become the first Black woman elected to the Senate.

As much as those women motivated me, I lacked any kind of power. Alone in my new city, I forced myself to repeat self-esteem mantras ("I am enough; I do enough; I have enough" were favorites despite none of it being true) as I hustled to the "L" train for interviews to land my first job. Thankfully, I got a modest offer within weeks—a receptionist role at a small advertising agency. Unfortunately, my dreams of brainstorming clever taglines would have to wait. Still, I convinced myself it wasn't a compromise—just a "pink collar" start. Never mind that I deplored pink.

With a mindless job, the toughest part of my day was determining what to wear in order to appear professional. This was no easy feat as my salary barely covered the necessities, and my closet was packed with preppy Chapel Hill staples: Duck Head shorts and wrinkle-free button-downs. I ultimately rotated my one pale green Ann Taylor suit, a beloved graduation gift from my successful older sister, throughout the week. I had learned from color theory textbooks (an increasing part of journalism school curriculum at the time) that pale green signifies immaturity, youthfulness and inexperience—so I was clearly dressed appropriately. There was no room for spilling coffee on myself as I wore the knee-length skirt on Mondays, Wednesdays and Fridays. My flexibility was in the pairings, alternating days with the matching double-breasted blazer, coordinating a silky (let's face it, polyester) Ann Taylor blouse and an ivory short-sleeved fitted crewneck sweater. My looks lacked imagination. I resembled a store mannequin. Today, I would be branded #basic. Two pairs of bland black Banana Republic trousers completed my sartorial schedule. Laundry day was critical; I ironed often. I craved a work uniform that showed I was serious, while I got coffee or made copies. I took it to heart when the hiring COO said, "You are the first person senior staff and clients see when entering the agency. And I promise you will be remembered when a job opens up." I glossed over his condescending commentary about my "nice, approachable face and voice." Don't forget "clever," I wanted to add.

Unfortunately, my independent career bravado did not translate into post-collegiate love. With instant bestsellers like *The Rules: Time-Tested Secrets for Capturing the Heart of Mr. Right*, girls needed much better role models. The tips were straight out of *I Love Lucy*: "Don't be funny," "Don't talk too much," and the most offensive advice to me, "Remember that you're dressing for men, not other women." The saddest part? Two women wrote that book. Fashion blogger "Man Repeller" (a.k.a. Leandra Medine) may have just been age seven at the time, but her concept of dressing for herself—and men be damned—was already alive and well in me. That is, if you can call wearing remnants from college making a statement.

No bestseller could sway what my mother imprinted on me about the importance of financial independence. She walked away from her sixteen-year marriage with just a Sears card. To get an apartment and her own Master Charge credit card, my father had to co-sign for her as if she were a teenager. "Never be in this position," she would say to me again and again. Sure, I had my own checking account. But even with a newly acquired second job, waiting tables in a bar each weekend, I barely met the bank minimum to keep it open. That changed a few years into my side hustle when I began grossing wads of cash. I would leave the bar at 2 a.m. strategically stuffing bills that I counted and organized face up into the pockets of my navy wide-leg palazzo pants from Art Effect, the cool boutique on Armitage I now permitted myself to enter, as I was also climbing the ranks in the ad world. (The front pockets of my white men's shirts came in handy on nights I scored big time with tips.) As Lincoln Park bars burped out drunk college kids, I hopped on my yellow Schwinn beach cruiser. Exhausted, I would pedal fast toward home, swerving to miss them. For the most part, I stuck to my pledge to deposit half the cash, allowing myself to buy clothes with the remainder. Amidst the bills, I occasionally found phone numbers of new acquaintances I'd met that night, and every so often, a boy who might want to go on a date with me.

I was so focused on earning money and my aspiring career that, along with dodging dinners out with girlfriends or flag football leagues on Saturdays, boys were not at the top of my agenda. Besides, they say dating in your twenties is like musical chairs. Or beds, depending on your style. I wanted no part of that. Sure, I humored some set-ups, but I always made sure to be back home for the start of *Party of Five*. I craved a great night's sleep—alone—before going to work. And despite morphing into an adult, I still shared a bedroom with a flight attendant who, while never home, left clothes, fragrance and makeup strewn all over our room. It reeked of Estée Lauder, as Jen was a tsunami of "Beautiful" perfume the rare times we crossed paths. My organized corner consisted of a twin bed. Sexy. (Although, according to *The Rules*, I was doing something right here, since having a single bed slyly showed suitors you were not plotting ahead for a future together.) Even if I'd had my own palatial bedroom, I was too busy to make a mess. I consistently held two jobs, at the ad agency and the bar, but I took on a third during the holidays. This was as much to buy myself clothes as it was for gifts. Applying to J. Crew was a no-brainer. I did not require training to fold using a clipboard; I'd employed this method since middle school. I welcomed customers who destroyed piles of sweaters. For me, nothing could be more cathartic than color coordinating them back into order. I would have made employee of the month if there was such an award. The employee discount (ten percent) was icing on the cake, lending itself to my style of gift giving: one for you, one for me. I was independent, driven and happy. Just me against the world.

Until JG swept me off my Keds.

Amidst warm beer and the cool art of the Old Town Art Fair in June of that year, I met a currency trader. He epitomized his native Iowa small town: big heart, friendly, and hard working. Despite netting a good income, he would tuck the right pants leg of his pressed khakis into his black dress sock each morning to bicycle downtown to the Mercantile Exchange. He waited tables on the side. He also saved money by having a roommate. JG and I had more than mere chemistry. We mirrored each other's values. He never pressured me to quit my bar job, despite the weekend hours away from him or attention from lecherous boys as I served rounds and rounds of Jägermeister shots. I felt seen and respected by JG from day one.

Raised by a strong mother and several older sisters, JG was more mature than any other twenty-something I'd encountered in Chicago. I mean, he was man enough to buy tampons at the store when I had the flu. He knew how to have deep conversations— about everything from our parents' divorces at an early age to stretch goals for our careers—and was self-assured enough to know that walking and talking in silence did not connote anger, but rather intimacy. Well before we celebrated a year anniversary, I began to dog ear Tiffany's ads in my issues of *Vogue*, *W*, *Glamour* and *Mademoiselle* magazines.

Our second jobs ultimately took a backseat to spending more time together and rejoining the friends and parties we had dropped with our rise in coupledom. We longed to drink from a red Solo cup. He missed bad keg beer. I couldn't wait to make small talk again with people who, unlike me, did "girls' nights." Hand in hand one night, we bundled up for the perfect Lincoln Park party. These were primarily held outside in the brisk late Fall temps around silver barrels of beer—along with the occasional break to traipse through a filthy kitchen to find a bathroom. Like all good couples, and at that time Gwyneth and Brad in particular, we dressed similarly. It just happens. We both wore khakis, although mine were far more pressed, and men's shirts, with mine, again, ironed to military crisp. Yet my pièce de resistance was a vintage chocolate brown suede jacket, courtesy of Una Mae's Freak Boutique, a secondhand store in Bucktown, a neighborhood that came into its own a few years later with the filming of the rom-com *High Fidelity*. There was an ease that came with being in love. I began branching out in my style with unique one-off pieces that matched my evolving identity: classic with an edge. I felt a rush when I first touched the soft suede in the boutique, but knew I'd struck gold when I turned it over to reveal a brilliant golden silk lining that had been disguised by the stack of battered Levi's.

One night, after we made our rounds at the party and caught up with friends, JG and I warmed up in the kitchen. Under bright fluorescent lighting, we leaned against (while simultaneously trying not to touch) the sticky counters rife with hastily poured shots and remnants of Drum roll-your-own cigarettes.

JG looked at me lovingly. "Nice pants," he said. "Where'd you get them?"

I lit up. I realized he was not saying this in jest. He really wanted to know. The khakis were a new purchase from Trina Turk that grazed above my ankle and hung beautifully, balancing baggy and fitted. They were expensive at $175 and required dry cleaning only (which made them even pricier), but I considered them a classic I'd wear for a long time. Not that I needed to justify it to myself, but according to my calculations, the cost-per-wear would make them a steal. The thrill for me was that I had never bought anything from Trina Turk before; her California ease and colorful vibe consisted more of Palm Beach prints than neutrals, so I had never gravitated towards her pieces in the past. But as I was earning more and now had an advertising job with an actual bonus, I found the oversized Gap clothes and blah Banana Republic apparel too ubiquitous. I sought garments that brought out greater individuality, and I strongly believed in investment pieces that mirrored where I wanted to go in the future. I saw these khakis, with their finer fabric, as the start of a wardrobe that had legs.

As we were about to head back out into the cold for a refill on our beers, JG touched the pants admiringly (or so I thought), and asked, "How much did those cost?" I was grateful he could tell they were expensive. He may have been inclined toward budgeting, but he also had good taste. While I initially thought there was no reason not to answer him truthfully, seeing his eyes roll when I stated the price, made me realize I had made a big mistake.

"For a pair of chinos?" he scoffed loudly.

"Khakis are not chinos" I retorted, matching his volume. I did not bother telling him that fashion could be a visual way to exercise your right to choose. Or that Trina Turk was a far cry financially from designer brands like Gucci which, under Tom Ford's tutelage was exploding since he began designing for the brand in 1994. I had recently watched in awe as pre-Goop Gwyneth shone at the 1996 MTV Awards in a red velvet tuxedo. I admired her and wanted a place to wear a velvet tux someday. But as the stale keg beer wafted in my nostrils, I felt deflated. We left the party, no longer hand in hand. Our silence no longer felt mature and self-assured, but stifling. Sleepless that night, I knew I could have easily separated myself from my clothes, but I wanted the freedom to know that I could splurge when I deemed it necessary. When I deserved it. When I had worked so damn hard, and I'd earned the right.

With my mother's lack of financial freedom replete with that Sears card visual on a mental loop, coupled with thinking about how hard women worked to become mens' equals, I could not let it go. Money is a feminist issue and wanting to be in control should create empowerment, not cause for apology. What started as an easy disagreement between JG and I festered over time, likely due to my growing resentment. I knew we would never make it. I could never stand for someone telling me what to wear. Or buy. Or ultimately, say. Trina had a motto: "You're full of life! Dress that way!" I had every right to do so. One of my design idols, Jil Sander, agreed. The famed minimalist designer who was spearheading a female takeover of fashion at that time—alongside my other bucket list designers Cynthia Rowley, Daryl Kerrigan and Ann Demeulemeester—once told *The New York Times*, "When I started, women were so devoted to dressing not for themselves but for somebody else. They were decorated—devoted to what I always call surface. Women have become so much stronger."

While I had matured with JG, I was far from fully formed. I mean, I was still hoarding college T-shirts. I thought of myself as a work in progress, just beginning to scratch the surface of who I wanted to become. Sure, I was finally rising up the ranks within the advertising world, now working at legendary agency Leo Burnett. But ultimately, my dream was to work in fashion. To break in, I would need to step out of the comforts of the Midwest. Those posh and pricey Trina Turk pants were my toe-in-the water. Clearly, JG had to swim elsewhere.

It was not an easy split, as I genuinely loved him. But sometimes, you have to prioritize the life you need over the love you want. When the breakup aftermath and loneliness set in, I wondered if I had made a mistake. (Not to mention, I couldn't find solace in wearing my lightweight Trina Turk khakis as brisk winter set in.) Was I being too hard on men? Could my criteria be too high—or too weird—in looking for a soul mate? That's the thing about being immature. You have no idea why your gut says to walk away, or stay away, from certain relationships, but you know deep down the decision is right. In fact, sometimes the harder it is to walk away, the more right the decision. I knew in the back—the way, way, way back—of my subconscious burned a desire to live an authentic life. A life where I could be vulnerable, where I deserved something more sophisticated and nuanced than this sweet small-town boy could give to me. What I had gained, and am so grateful to JG for, is the confidence I gleaned from my decision to end it. L'Oréal had been right all along: I was worth it.

Once single, I began filling my time with writing. I completed my first personal essay two weeks after the breakup. Coincidentally, and perhaps tellingly, the piece wasn't about JG at all; it was about my career and the desire to leave the advertising agency world for good. I had a wanderlust that I couldn't put my finger on, but I knew I was different. It was more than fashion or my lack of desire to fit in with the measured lifestyle of the Central Time Zone. I was meant for bigger things, bolder clothes. Moving was the only option—and the best way to ensure I wouldn't fall back into JG's arms. I packed my pristinely pressed Trina Turk khakis and left for New York City a year later.

While my heart would occasionally wander back to JG throughout my first year in New York, my mind focused on finding my way, both with the haphazard street grid system (Why the hell was everything so confusing below 14th Street?) and with who I wanted to be. There were no cell phones yet. I relied on laminated trifold maps that mocked my naiveté, thinking I could easily start over in another big city alone. Streetwise maps for the unwise girl. At least I had learned not to pull them out at the top of the subway stairs. (I'd initially infuriated hundreds of already incensed commuters with this amateur tactic.) Lost in this city of dreams, it didn't matter what I wore. I had become invisible. The irony was that at nearly thirty I finally understood Aristotle's sentiment, "The more you know, the more you realize you don't know."

My closet screamed, "aimless." When your kitchenette stove serves as storage for alternate season shoes, there's literally no room to hold onto the past. Yet, I was hoarding emotions along with grunge artifacts and a Marshall Field's pants suit. Sure, my wardrobe was ironed, color coordinated and hanging from matching clear hangers I took from the aerobics store I worked at in high school. (The Home Edit would have been proud.) Still, my closet was schizophrenic. Leftovers from omnipresent Gap and Banana Republic stood out as painfully average in the start of a new, "look at me" wardrobe. I shopped for the woman I longed to become, courtesy of sample sales at DVF, Theory and Tocca. I straddled two worlds, triumphant in neither. I profoundly felt what Stacy London, the stylist and fashion guru who made us laugh and learn with the famed show *What Not to Wear,* liked to say: "Holding on to who you were doesn't serve who you're going to be."

Fact: a significant shift in our lives shows up in how we get dressed. Even Virginia Woolf believed fashion plays a role in our outlook: "Vain trifles as they seem, clothes have, they say, more important offices than merely to keep us warm. They change our view of the world and the world's view of us." Resigned to let go of my past and eager to see things differently, I assembled a pile of formerly loved garments that represented my twenties to donate at Housing Works thrift shop, my favorite non-profit designed to help those living with AIDs. I needed a clean slate.

With the notorious Trina Turk pants dangling prominently in the center of the eight-foot garment rod, my now nearly vacant closet was wide open for new things. My heart and head, now free from clutter, felt open to new possibilities as well. As the architect of my own life, I realized I did have the power to make myself happy. I was confident that with my first investment—a "Breaking into Women's Magazines" writing class at The New School—I would find joy and feel less engulfed by the city. I hoped to find my voice so I could be seen—and *heard.*

FOUR

You Never Forget Your First
in Ann Demeulemeester

IN 2001, when *Saturday Night Live* parodied Jeffrey's—one of the first boutiques to stock avant-garde designers like Dries Van Noten and Alexander McQueen—it reflected reality more than comedy. Jeffrey Kalinsky hadn't just transformed New York's Meatpacking District into a luxury fashion destination, replacing chilled sides of beef with floor-to-ceiling displays of chic runway garments, he made shopping feel exclusive. Like a nightclub with a forbidding red rope, Jeffrey's was all about pre-approval and fitting in. At the time, I just peered in the windows. But I aspired to walk in with my head held high like a regular.

I'd been initiated into rarified retail in Chicago a few years earlier. *Women's Wear Daily* once declared, "Every city needs its own Jeffrey or Colette—or at least a store that, for lack of a better description, compares itself to those two groundbreaking retailers." Chicago had one. That mononymous trailblazer was Blake in Lincoln Park. While the picturesque neighborhood got its name from more than 1,200 acres of green space, the heart of the community was its low-key bars and boutiques. It was a mecca for millions of us post grads trying to find our way in the world. But Blake wasn't low-key—it was low profile, by design. It teetered on obscurity as founders Marilyn Blaszka and Dominic Marcheschi approached retail like Bungalow 8, Amy Sacco's legendary New York City nightclub in the mid-aughts. There was no branded signage. Even today, nothing says highbrow louder than an obscure entrance. But this heralded force in fashion's inaccessibility and aversion to publicity, were more than made up for by originality and a loyalty to Belgian designers.

Years before I even peered into Jeffrey's, I spent my hard-earned waitressing tips on Chicago's Armitage Street—frequenting boutiques like Cynthia Rowley and Art Effect, but only ever walking past Blake's strikingly bare display windows. "When will I have the courage to walk in?" I'd mutter to myself. It wasn't like I dressed in thigh-high boots like *Pretty Woman*'s hooker-with-a-heart-of-brass Vivian Ward. (Though, with the wad of cash I earned bartending back then, I probably could've passed for a stripper.) Unlike shopping at agnès b. and Barneys where you felt discreet, entering Blake's domain required more than just money. The imported merchandise at the exclusive store seemed to demand a mortgage, a significant other, a chic destination in life. Or, at the very least, a subscription to international issues of *Vogue*. (And this was years before Blake was named the eighth most expensive store in America and crowned one of Gwyneth's favorites on goop). The only thing I owned outright back then was my aforementioned trusty yellow Schwinn beach cruiser and some hand-me-down luggage.

Before I relocated to the fashion capital, I knew I needed a wardrobe that matched my oversized ambitions. I'd landed a vice president, account director job in New York—and was even being moved by the advertising agency, Saatchi & Saatchi—but a job in fashion or a byline in *Vogue* was ultimately on my grand to-do list. Maybe I would add publishing a fashion essay collection? NBD. I knew my minimalist cardigans would make a small mark in the Big Apple, so I had to open my mind—and my wallet—before I moved. After nine years of wearing out the sidewalk in front of Blake, I decided that going in couldn't be harder than moving solo across the country. Then again, I'd never wavered in my decision to move to New York City. Hooked on the first season of *Sex and the City*, I couldn't help but picture myself as Carrie Bradshaw—what girl didn't at the start of the series?—as I was chasing love and a career in fashion (not necessarily in that order). Bound by a budget for nearly a decade, it was time to break free of sartorial shackles and make a purchase before the stakes (and my rent) skyrocketed.

I took a deep breath and yanked open Blake's substantial door. An echo boomed across the high ceilings and pristine white walls. I felt at home with the immaculate space and sterile scent, but it was awkward to be alone in the store. Donning a uniform that felt elevated but suited for the brisk Fall weather, I wore an ecru J.Crew rollneck sweater layered over a black slip dress and paired with black Doc Martens. I cautiously approached the first table, covered in unfamiliar, expertly curated garments. They seemed casually arranged to my untrained eye, but each one felt intentional. A sea of knits in rich but muted tones: gray, plum, navy. The labels, though—those I recognized: Jil Sander, Martin Margiela, Dries Van Noten, Ann Demeulemeester. I visually mused over each garment before reaching for the last one, a char-coal gray knit. It was bulky despite its soft wool fabric. I loved that contrast. As I picked it up to hold it up against me, it unfurled... and kept unfurling. Six feet of fabric unraveled like a parody of the Constitution. Or a CVS receipt. Before I could even fumble to remerchandise it, a lithe woman swathed in a rich, ankle grazing bordeaux dress with a black embroidered sweater ("Dries Van Noten," she would later snip at me, unsolicited) appeared at my side.

"Ann Demeulemeester. Isn't it spectacular?" she asked. Rhetorically I assumed. I had no idea who she spoke of, nor could I ever pronounce that name—even at gunpoint. And what the hell was this massive sheet of wool that nearly draped to my ankles? Where was Jacques when I needed him most?

My haughty helper explained that the garment was a dress. "Five armholes allow it to wrap around the body for an interesting silhouette. It's versatile with layered parts and falling panels," she said with exacting exuberance.

"Like a toga!" I almost blurted but had enough couth to keep to myself.

She then handed me what appeared to be a worksheet, a faint photocopy with a size eight handwritten font, displaying a quintet of sketches illustrating various ways to wear the dress. She looked to me for an enthusiastic reaction. Frozen, as if I were heavily Botoxed, I managed a polite smile.

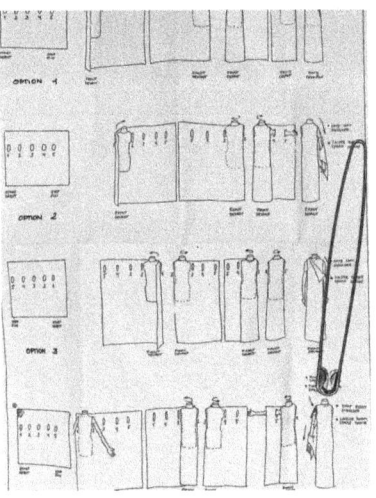

Five Armholes. Infinite Possibilities. Wore them all.

While there were no cell phone cameras or selfies to commemorate this moment, I will never forget my Demeulemeester dealer helping me out of my sweater and winding the wool sheet around me. The "dress," as odd as it may have appeared initially, was spectacular. Unusual, but cool. She informed me coolly that this, my first true luxury purchase, was considered a fashion UFO—alien and mysterious to most but open to infinite styling interpretations by beloved avant-garde purists. Before glancing at the handwritten price tag, I'd made the decision to go bankrupt if necessary. Rather than scrutinize the styling cues in the store, I hurried to pay. I had to get home and explore the options. Play dress up. As Blake's devoured a sizable portion of my checking account, I was bestowed with an exceptionally large matte silver diaper pin. The Demeulemeester dress itself was carefully slid into a garment bag that prominently featured the name. No logo, of course.

"I nearly forgot to show you the accessory," said the luxury label lover, pointing at the pin. The accessory, both functionally chic yet unconventional, was typical of the innovative Belgian designer who was notorious for challenging traditional garment construction. "It's not necessary to use it, as the diagrams show," she said, pointing to the how-to-wear cheat sheet. "Get creative with it."

"Oh, I will," I replied with a smile that she didn't bother to return.

Still, I felt a quiet sense of validation as I sailed out of Blake. Buying my first Ann Demeulemeester was unforgettable, but over the past twenty-seven years as I've worn this exceptional dress in all its variations—each time reflecting my creativity and evolving style—it's served as a reminder that I had belonged at Blake all along. It was also the armor I needed for New York. I was leaving the very next day.

As I approached my flight, I focused more on the Blake garment bag I was carrying than on the life I was leaving behind. Crossing over the jetway, I looked past first class for my seat, 16C. The flight attendant glanced down at the brand name draped over my arm. Her demeanor shifted as she leaned toward me and said in a hushed tone, "Anything from Blake should hang up here in first class." As I handed over my prized possession, her counterpart sidled up and said, "You should stay close by. Why don't you take seat 2A?" I wasn't even wearing the dress yet and already felt the weight of my aspirations aligning with reality.

I tipped the movers at 4:30 p.m. that afternoon and shut the door behind them. Thirty boxes stared back at me in my new apartment, nestled between an Aveda Salon and where John Lennon was shot on the Upper West Side. Despite years of living solo in Chicago, I'd never felt so alone. I knew growth required more than a shift in geography and an elevated wardrobe. Half of me was still safely enveloped in bubble wrap, clinging to the familiar. The other half was eagerly awaiting discovery. I unpacked until sunrise. Then—with two days left before starting my new job at the agency responsible for the relocation—I set out to shed my lingering Midwest persona. I'd never chased a celeb hairstyle. I'd dodged the Rachel and resisted the Dorothy Hamill wedge, even under elementary school pressure. But after watching *Sliding Doors* earlier that year, I couldn't stop thinking about Gwyneth Paltrow's iconic post-breakup haircut. Exhausted but resolute, I wandered into SoHo looking for a similar transformation.

"What do you think?" asked the chic stylist as he swiveled me around.

Staring back at me was a girl with short hair. Ten inches of enviable Sarah Jessica Parker curls had been shorn to a pixie cut; I had become my own UFO. Coco Chanel was right: "A woman who cuts her hair is about to change her life." I had come this far. Now, without long hair to hide behind, I had no choice but to keep going. Like Ann Demeulemeester, I was done playing it safe.

FIVE

Saying Goodbye Too Soon in OshKosh

NEW YORKERS' proclivity for wearing all black traces in part, back to the late '70s and '80s when Americans began admiring minimalist clothes from inspiring Japanese designers such as Issey Miyake, Rei Kawakubo and Yohji Yamamoto. The fashion was forward-thinking, powerful and—meaningful to a city that over-values weight—slimming. Ever aspiring to possess these traits, I donned the fashionable funeral look frequently. Yet when it came time to bury my father, I had nothing to wear.

Diehard New Yorkers believe in the ten-year rule: it takes a decade to become a full-fledged New Yorker. However, I thought it took a decade for your wardrobe to evolve from a few little black dresses into a sea of black. Despite embodying minimalism and a love of neutrals in Chicago, black had never been a head-to-toe staple for me—the one thing I had in common with Anna Wintour, who reportedly hates all black wardrobes. The irony is that I moved to New York City in 1998 just after the fall fashion shows where Donna Karan, Calvin Klein and Helmut Lang put color on the runway. The city was aghast. Even famed fashion editor Suzy Menkes reported it felt "off key" to witness a saturated palette parade down the runway for the upcoming spring season.

As much as I wanted to fit into my new city and flourish

enough to break into fashion, I recalled what the late Gianni Versace—who had been killed one year prior—once said, "Be yourself. It's the only fashion you can wear; it's you." Inspired by this sentiment, I showed up on my fourth day at the agency in a vintage pantsuit purchased a few days earlier, during my first exploration in Soho. I knew the orange and black windowpane wool suit was bold, but I felt confident given the flawless fit. What did I have to lose, I thought? I had just cut all my hair off. "Cool suit. Looks just like my grandmother's couch," said a young account executive sarcastically, as I walked off the elevator. I witnessed several eyerolls before I took cover in my office for most of the day.

Even today, I don't know why I thought I had what it took to pull off the Halloween-esque suit. It seemed chic, but really, the look screamed "period-piece actor." Despite trying to "beg off" (a British colloquialism for squirming out of an obligation, which I picked up quickly working at the U.K. ad agency) I was forced to join an office drinks outing in my carnival ensemble. Arriving at the hip bar The Ear Inn, where a letter of the neon sign was burnt out, I feared someone might suggest replacing it with some of my suit fabric. As a new hire, I drank for free. As you can imagine, that's a dangerous discount. Within the hour, I'd been served more than I could handle—and finished every glass. I knew I had to escape before I embarrassed myself, but an Irish goodbye in bright orange was out of the question. I quickly slurred "so long" and ran for a cab. Minutes later, I vomited in my handbag as I headed uptown—and after riffling through the sickness, I realized I had no cash.

I asked the annoyed driver to pull over at an ATM across from my apartment. But it suddenly dawned on me that I didn't even know my PIN yet. I had to make a junior executive decision. The cab driver and I locked eyes before I ran, my flamboyant orange and black jacket billowing as I hustled across lanes of traffic. Horns honked. Drivers grumbled. "You a bad lady!" I heard my cab driver scream multiple times before I opened the 500-pound door to my lobby. (He was right. I was also a "badly dressed lady.") I was never more relieved to see the seventy-five-year-old front desk clerk of my pre-war building. She looked at me with mercy and said, "Get a good night's rest, dear." While nursing a severe hangover the following day, I replayed the scene over and over—the cab, the sprint, the orange suit, the shame. That's when it hit me: I was officially a New Yorker. Not because I skipped out on cab fare (though, guilty) or because I vowed not to wear colorful clothes again (also guilty), but because I survived it, despite being mortified, and kept going.

Obviously, I never wore that vintage suit again—and I stopped trying so hard to assert a new unfamiliar style. Instead, I leaned in on my trusted essentials: button downs, crewneck cashmere sweaters and trousers that had worked for me in Chicago. I invested in—and wore as often as possible—a basic, but beautifully tailored, black dress from Mayle in Nolita. I didn't want to stand out. I wanted to figure out how to fit in. As I was finding my way, midriff-baring Y2K style was hitting stores. *Vogue* had declared a new sequel of supermodels—Shalom Harlow, Kirsty Hume, Stella Tennant and Amber Valletta among them—and fashion became increasingly playful, color-laden and high tech. Newer fibers like PVC made miniskirts and blazers feel futuristic. The rise on pants dropped, while shirts got cropped—if for no other reason than to show all the navel rings. The closer we got to the possible apocalypse, the more fashion worsened. I dabbled in low rise jeans and "going out" tops on weekends but otherwise buckled down into staid minimalism as if to hold on tight. This too shall pass, I thought.

I had read enough fashion magazines to know black is not only the cool uniform, but it makes you look more pulled together—and expensive. Even on a paltry budget like mine. I bought black turtlenecks from The Gap in bulk. They complemented my short hair. (I missed my phantom long curls less with something against the nape of my neck.) And while everyone from *Vogue* to Gap were hyping turtlenecks that season, I loved the garment's historical significance. Feminist powerhouses like Gloria Steinem and Angela Davis wore them while trailblazing in the early '70s. The famed Chicagoan photographer Victor Skrebneski, who I knew from my receptionist days in the Windy City, had created the "black turtleneck sweater portraits" with celebs from Andy Warhol and Truman Capote to Carolina Herrera and Bette Davis wearing the classic staple. While the turtleneck was often paired with black trousers, I also found myself wearing them with OshKosh overalls on casual Fridays, a concept that had been gaining momentum across the country. I worked on the OshKosh brand while in Chicago. Having spent a significant amount of time at their home base of Wisconsin shooting their campaigns, I snagged a pair before they stopped making the utilitarian denim for adults in 1997. To me, the brand embodied wholesomeness and conjured up images of families piling into Wagoneers and playing flag football over Thanksgiving. Then again, maybe I just watched too much *Friends*. Rachel Green was notorious for wearing overalls, after all. The denim cut made me miss my family.

I'd lived in New York less than two months when the panicked call arrived: "Dad had a stroke." His prognosis was not good, and according to the doctor, the end could come within seventy-two hours. At that moment, it did not matter that we had an impassive relationship and that he did not know—or under-stand—the woman I had become. Within hours, I swerved into the parking lot. As I entered the hospital room, I braced myself for the worst. With a newly shaved head and a complete loss of verbal skills, he was screaming inaudible phrases as a team of nurses tried to restrain him. Bucking like an animal, he twisted and pulled to free himself from both the bed and the immobilized life his brain injury had given him.

I sat by his side for hours before he was wheeled into surgery. I felt overwhelmed by my selfish thoughts and the angst that I would never forgive myself if he died on the operating table. How could he go before I had the chance to tell him how I really felt?

Considering our history of poor communication, I didn't imagine that talking with each other would be any easier once my father survived the operation. Our twenty-nine-year relationship played in my mind as I stood outside of his room waiting for the nurses to change his bedding. Our rare heart-to-hearts had always stemmed from a crisis, like the end of my parents' marriage two decades earlier or the scare years ago when he'd learned of his chemical imbalance.

When he survived the procedure, I knew I had a second chance. I thought he may never speak again, but we could heal. That emotional suture would call for time and consistency. So, I fled my New York office promptly at 5 p.m. each following Friday, breaking a sweat to get to Penn Station to take the Amtrak to Baltimore. I sat at my father's bedside throughout each weekend. My sister in Australia would call on occasion, given the sixteen-hour time difference, to check in as she kicked off her weekend. On the train platform, I spoke in hushed tones despite the booming Happy Hour surrounding me and the loud crack of beers opening. As a regular on the Northeast Corridor rail, I grew familiar with passengers at Penn Station but never spoke to a soul. I didn't want to discuss my life—or lack thereof.

Since moving to New York two months earlier, I had not accomplished much of anything and felt lost. I lived to spend time next to my father, even if only to receive a cold stare and hold a warm limp hand. His blank gaze seldom broke, although he frequently mustered the energy to retaliate against the nurses. He refused to eat and began biting the nurses that struggled to pry open his mouth for "enticing" foods like hospital Jell-O. "Hey, Mikey. He likes it!" he once exclaimed in a clear voice as he pushed away yet another dinner. It was like he was mocking the nurses and informing the world that his inability to speak did not make him an invalid. While I was not certain my dad could under-stand my words, I believed these visits were my opportunity to tell him about my new life in Manhattan, the writing class I had recently started, and the end of the relationship with a man I once hoped would become my husband. I knew he heard me; I felt he understood what I was saying. He mustered a smile when I assured him there was plenty of time for him to regain strength to one day walk me down the aisle.

The Original White Shirt Hero.

When he finally did find the strength to form words, I stared intently at his mouth. "Priorities...forgetting...me," was all I could decipher. He could mutter only a few words at first, but as I continued to listen to what he could say—often between long pauses—I nodded. He carefully enunciated to express himself, telling me things he had wanted to say years ago but had held back. It was our encore to express the love and care we'd always had but were too proud and stubborn to reveal. Like me, he felt it had been easier to relate from a distance. Like me, he wished he had realized the importance of our relationship. Like me, he wanted to forget the misgivings of our past and instead begin to confide in each other.

Overwhelmed by my emotions, I climbed over the protective bed railing to hug him harder and stronger than I ever had. His fragile arms struggled, and he let out a sigh as he held onto me with his limited strength. I knew somewhere inside his scrambled brain remained the man that brought me into the world, who loved me the best way that he knew how. As we cried, my dad and I realized we were not shedding tears of pain, but tears of joy knowing that we had found our way back.

I returned to my apartment with hope. But it was short-lived. Each time my mother called, I got rattled. Did my dad regress? My gut instinct was not optimistic. One morning a few days after settling back home in the city, I answered a call from my mom with, "What happened?" He was going back into surgery, she told me, and I needed to come right away. I grabbed the gym bag from beneath my desk, filled with Adidas sweats and a college T-shirt I'd worn threadbare as pajamas for the past decade. Unsurprisingly clad in my uniform of OshKosh overalls and a black turtleneck, I boarded the Amtrak.

He was gone the next afternoon.

I was prepared to visit my father, not bury him. The next few days, I struggled with what to wear. I had nothing black in tow, except for the well-worn Gap turtleneck, which was inadequate. As I helped pick out a casket, wrote the newspaper obituary and awaited my sister's arrival from Australia, I scoured my mother's closet. I could not, as Miranda once said on *Sex and the City* when her own mom died, "buy a shitty black dress I'll never wear again." There was no time. My sister, the perpetual over packer, would likely arrive with something for me, I mused, but she needed to land in time; the flight from Australia was twenty hours and five minutes. There was not a minute to spare. We had yet to tell her Dad passed away. It was too much for her to handle alone, and we feared she may want to drink herself to oblivion in the air to stomach the grief.

"I'm at the American Express counter and they are not letting me on a bereavement flight," Lisa said. "It would be different if he had passed away already."

"He is going to die before you arrive," I lied unconvincingly before bursting into tears. My mother grabbed the phone.

"Sweetheart, just get on a flight. You need to arrive right away. We will handle the cost," she said, her voice calm and filled with grace.

"Let me see what I can do," Lisa said.

Before I could restrain my escalating grief, I grabbed the cordless phone and screamed, "HE'S DEAD. HE'S ALREADY DEAD. PLEASE COME HOME NOW!" My voice breaking as I spat out the words. I had not meant to be cruel, but I could not lie to her anymore. American Express came through and she boarded, arriving to us the following day with smeared makeup and bloodshot eyes, but sober and stricken with grief. After suffocating her with hugs, I ransacked her luggage. She, of course, had something black I could borrow.

I retired my OshKosh overalls after the funeral. I could not look at them without recalling climbing into his hospital bed, his hand clutching a buckle loop to keep me from falling out.

My father was like my overalls in many ways. He was a go-to that I had not relied on for years but ultimately leaned on for comfort when I was lost. They were both the embodiment of American goodness. Wearing the overalls repeatedly would never bring back the idyllic upbringing I dreamed of but never had. Nor would my OshKosh bring back the dad who I lost too early, at age fifty-nine.

A few years after his death, OshKosh briefly began making overalls for adults again. Even though they were back in fashion and played a role in the emerging style of high-low dressing, I could not bear to buy a new pair.

The Aughts

SIX

Wearing My Heart on My
Cynthia Rowley Sleeve

OIL OF OLAY, the pink beauty fluid our foremothers first slathered on in 1952, changed its identity at the turn of the twenty-first century. Weighed down by the word "oil"—which was not yet the indispensable beauty essential it is today—and multiple iterations across the globe (Olay, Olaz, Ulay, Ulan), the brand set out to become the Madonna of skincare. A mononym. A single moniker designed to seduce women browsing the congested beauty aisle and make them love themselves. I witnessed the Olay transformation firsthand, thanks to my extraordinary job at Saatchi & Saatchi as the vice president, account director working on upstream innovation and the future of the brand's portfolio. But, while I appeared successful (and well hydrated) on the outside, inside I still felt so unworthy.

My British employer—no longer just an advertising agency, but officially an "ideas company"—was Olay's significant other, developing marketing campaigns and its striking identity. But my CEO, Kevin Roberts, knew it was more than that. He'd devised a branding breakthrough called "lovemarks," believing that love is the way forward for business and that only through profound emotional connection with consumers can brands survive long term. I was honored to partner with the inventive Procter &

Gamble team as we strove to earn what Roberts called "loyalty beyond reason" and fulfill, what he deemed, one of business' primary functions: to make the world a better place.

Creating a lovemark that is built on respect and love, takes work. I was passionate about the beauty business and coincidentally had no love life of my own, so I threw myself into the process with elation. I brimmed with ambition and hoped my former "I'm worth it" mantra, which had been trodden by tough bosses and romantic rejections, would reemerge. There had been no love marking (or making, for that matter) in my social life for a while. The Olay assignment turned out to be the antidote. The collaboration enhanced my self-esteem (like new boyfriends once did) and I knew we were making a difference in the world by focusing on empowerment and self-acceptance, rather than (the usual) unattainable beauty standards. We struck a chord with women around the world who were tired of being told they needed fixing, and the shift had a ripple effect on the industry. I spent most of my waking hours with a Cincinnati-based brand team who became like family to me.

Still, the work added up as we developed new product ideas and mapped strategic positioning for Olay's portfolio over the next two to ten years. Seventy-hour workweeks blurred into one another as we chanted the new campaign's rallying cry—"Love the Skin You're In!"—from city to city, testing concepts and listening closely during focus groups with women. It's crazy to think that something as basic as washcloths (a.k.a. "daily facials") and department store moisturizers—now easy to grab on a spree at Target thanks to the new "masstige" category Total Effects created—could lift a discontented New Yorker's spirits. But it wasn't the products themselves that truly sunk in; it was the unfiltered stories and quiet moments between pitches.

While I dreamed of–and sometimes had nightmares about— the campaign's "7 Signs of Aging," it was the conversations with women (everywhere from Germany and London to Iowa and Los Angeles) that seeped into my skin. They were open and vulnerable about how they saw themselves, their fears and hopes, what they needed—from their skincare *and* their lives. In those moments, I realized something fundamental: We all crave the same thing: love. We shaped new concepts around those needs, which was good for business. And the lengthy discussions about life became therapy for me. Without the co-pay. Or the couch.

One week, we holed up in a conference room in London, which boasted a view of the world's biggest Ferris wheel (the "Big Eye"), but appeared like every other conference room in the world. Four windowless walls replete with papers and product samples strewn about, generic beige furniture, and side tables overflowing with water bottles and the token stainless steel coffee carafe that never truly kept the watery brew hot. Prepackaged sandwiches tasted the same regardless of which side of the pond we were meeting on. While bantering about how far women go to feel good about their skin, I blurted out, "When I get Botox, it makes me feel..." The brand manager cut me off.

"You're only thirty-two!" he exclaimed.

"That's so New York of you," laughed the marketing director.

Even then, I was not shy about being one of the 1.6 million people who currently get Botox. Despite my initial hesitation to be injected by a toxin, I had become nonchalant about this fountain of youth in its off-label use. Botox was like a sample sale find: not everyone had access to it and the results brought me unparalleled joy. I rarely considered that I was too young, only that I was eager to thwart the dreaded "11" imprint between my eyebrows, brought on my natural born scowl. It didn't help that my mother noted that my glower might be the reason I was approached less by men than my sister, who had a more affable face. My brutally honest mother would have gone as far as to say I had RBF— "resting bitch face"—but that concept didn't become part of the vernacular until more than a decade later, in 2013, thanks to a viral video from the witty comedy group, "Broken People."

My foray into Botox was smooth. The previous year, I had visited an up-and-coming Tribeca dermatologist for an innocuous skin issue: whiteheads reappeared each fall on the back of my arm, like the latest trend showing up in time for Fashion Week. Sitting in a waiting room that resembled the Design Within Reach catalog, I thought, "this office is too chic for my ailment." My suspicion was confirmed when the young, hot Indian doctor, sporting what looked like Jil Sander, looked me over—and not in a medical diagnostic way. I felt self-conscious and wished I had dressed better for the appointment.

Since the closet purge years prior, I had begun cultivating a wardrobe that proudly represented me, but rent, which usurped sixty percent of my income, often got in the way. I preferred to meet a friend to stand in line for a sample sale than to sit down at a bar for a pricey glass of Pinot. We'd talk fast to catch up before rushing into a warehouse or cramped showroom to scour bins for Prada coats, DVF dresses or anything from Theory, a brand I loved as much for the more accessible price as the ability to wear from the office to an evening out. But money was tight. I often relied on former staples—my tomboy approach to feminine—as I had that day at the dermatologist. Twenty years later, I learned that former *Vogue* editor and retailer Ann Mashburn coined this look "unisexy." Meaning, if a pair of proper trousers and even the most well-worn men's shirt brought you confidence, it was a look that said, "go ahead and stare." Knowing this could have helped me stand a little taller that day in the swank Tribeca office.

While my black flat-front trousers and starched navy fitted men's shirt may have lacked visual interest, I looked to shoes to make a statement. But at that moment even my chic, black, über-pointy kitten heels felt like stiletto training wheels that screamed "I take the subway." It felt like I was underdressed for a date, rather than perfectly prepared for a derm appointment. Me with my bumpy flesh, which the hot doctor later diagnosed as "chicken skin." Forget fashion, I thought. Skin diseases are quite the turn-off.

But it was not just what I wore that was unnerving me. The way the hot doctor stared through me made me squirm after he gave me exfoliating cream and advice to get rid of the poultry problem. "You should consider Botox," he said offhandedly, as if ordering a sandwich. (Not likely, as his physique screamed "no carbs.") I may not have looked dynamic and, unfortunately, I did rely on baby oil and tin foil to aggressively tan in the sun as a teen. But hey, I didn't look that bad. Or did I? Plus, I knew about skincare thanks to my job. I had a phenomenal product allowance for research and knew brands were being developed to treat the "11" topically. I also knew Botox had yet to be approved by the FDA. It was only being used as a non-FDA application for wrinkles for celebrities; the real victory for the brand was its initial success fixing eye disorders and cervical pain. But what did I have to lose? Oh yeah, my resting bitch face.

With my pair of forming lines erased, I looked months younger. As more of a preventative measure, no one—not even myself, despite spending far too much time staring into a magnifying mirror over the next week—noticed the subtle shift. I may not have been able to see much difference on my own face, but I had enough vision to know Botox was destined for the rest of the country after that first visit. I was vocal about it with the Procter & Gamble team. "Everyone wants what celebs have. Botox works, if you can get past the fact that it's poison. It will be in malls, like ear piercing, before you know it," I confidently proclaimed.

DESPITE MY TAUTER FACE, I still preferred to frequent an old dive bar, Peters. It was four stumbling blocks from my apartment and played decent music like Foo Fighters and The Counting Crows. But its best quality was proximity to a movie theatre, the second largest grossing box office in the country, where I often escaped if the night out for drinks was just too taxing. I saw everything that was released but leaned hard on rom coms. There'd been a boom in the genre (including meaningful soundtracks, which I played on repeat). I couldn't get enough of anything featuring Meg Ryan and felt incredibly seen by Bridget Jones. I may have been more successful (and more fit) than Bridget Jones, but the usually lithe Renée Zellweger was magnetic on screen and made the character relatable. Her rendition of *"All by Myself"* was more than a song; it was my anthem. Mostly, I just needed to see less of the four walls of my apartment. I had finally admitted to myself that being alone had gotten lonely. Still, I refused to lower my standards. Not even Botox could disguise my disdain when losers or drunks sidled up to me at the bar.

A few months after my injections, as I regained movement in my forehead, I found myself creating laugh lines when I met AJ, a guy with more charisma than anyone I'd encountered in a long time. It was a cold, snowy night and after hours of shameless flirting, he walked me home under the pretense of being a gentleman. "It's on my way," he mused. Our hands dangled close as we walked, grazing as if they might want to one day interlock. As we sidestepped heaps of discarded Christmas trees lining the sidewalks for trash day, I told him about my own dried-up Fraser fir, now a fire hazard in my apartment given its proximity to a radiator. He offered to carry it down the next day—if we could have lunch first. I wanted to swoon but reserved the right to be cautious. I was tired of directionless dating and had lived on the Upper West Side long enough to know Jewish boys don't typically end up with Christians like me. Girls with an Italian heritage and a confirmation name. But AJ seemed different, so just as I would examine the ingredients on a beauty package before deciding, I needed to know a little more of what was inside him before I got involved.

"You want to help with my Christmas tree? Just what any Jewish mother wants to see!" I said sarcastically.

"It's hard enough to find love, without letting religion get in the way," he said smiling, as his eyes crinkled with joy.

AJ's humor and adoration were just the injection I needed. I'd been solo for so long and had forgotten how good it felt to see myself through someone's loving gaze. Since arriving in New York, my bed mates had been back issues of *Vogue* and *W*, the oversized glossy that could "knock someone out" according to the China doll-sized, elderly woman responsible for handing me my mail. (She said the same thing each month.) Its grand size paled in comparison to its rich content; I scoured the magazine dreaming of one day actually seeing fashion shows *on* the runway, instead of on the pages. I loved to wake up and finish a section of the hefty magazine, still tucked under my covers, before heading out for coffee.

That lunch with AJ morphed into all-day movie watching on my couch, ordering in dinner and a subsequent workweek flurry of emails and calls to see each other again. My beloved magazines got relegated to the bedside table—of course, stacked by date. I vowed to read them cover to cover another time. The ease with which AJ and I slid into a relationship was incomparable; I had grown up significantly—in years and wisdom—since dating J. Losing my father a few years prior had been a large part of maturing as well. I felt comfortable being myself with this lovely new man, showcasing my silly side, sharing family secrets and telling stories about goals without fear of judgement. He embraced it all.

AJ's open religious views were not his only calling card. A classic New York City boy with more brains than height, he had an edge, dry wit, and social life primed to include me. As a member of a private social club where he spent significant time hosting drinks and playing squash (very Waspy of him), he made sure our calendar brimmed with activities. My dry-cleaning bill doubled as I finally had the opportunity to wear more sophisticated dresses (my DFV wrap and Miu Miu bubble dress, in particular) I'd acquired at sample sales over the years. Until then, I'd held off wearing them as life did not feel important enough to don dresses of that caliber. We were still a decade away from memes of someone strolling a grocery aisle in a ballgown—reminding us to wear everything we own. To date, my favorite is artist Mary Engelbreit's motto: "Don't ever save anything for a special occasion. Being alive is the special occasion." With AJ, I rose to the occasion. Falling in love will do wonders for your skin, my derm said on my following visit. "And your wardrobe," I retorted with a laugh.

While we swooned, AJ encountered some career turmoil. It made him vulnerable and more affectionate, leaning on me who loved nothing more than to nurture. A natural-born cheerleader, I embraced the shift. Simultaneously, my Olay role continued to expand, and with it came more travel. My time with AJ was limited and precious. As summer hit, we ventured to Amagansett for a long weekend. Both of us needed the break from the city; time apart was drawing a wedge. AJ stressed about upcoming interviews and, despite disguising it, the length of time since his last paycheck. As he sunned on the beach with friends, I stole away to the Cynthia Rowley boutique for an afternoon event. AJ knew I was crazy for the designer, who had been the sole source of whimsy in my closet since living in Chicago. But it had been more than her originality and proximity to my after-agency hours bar job—where I left with bulging pockets of cash eager to be spent on clothes—that led me to Cynthia Rowley's store. I gravitated to her moxie. Cynthia launched her business with $3,000 and a dream. I admired her. To me, she was the exemplar for following creative aspirations. I cherished the garments I had purchased, like the feminine schoolgirl dresses worn on repeat to Lincoln Park bars and art fairs, printed pants I'd pair with my trusty white, well-pressed shirts for work and play. I loved breezing through her boutique on Armitage and discovering new items every season. Her brand just embodied FUN.

Nothing had changed when I walked into her store in East Hampton for the event nearly five years later. I was mesmerized by her continued fascination with color. The flirty store design was decked out with powder blue stenciled walls, vintage-inspired floral upholstery and stacks of rainbow striped books, her recent venture created alongside her best friend Ilene Rosenzweig, a former style editor at *The New York Times*. In the few years since they'd launched the Swell brand with the cheeky debut book,

Swell: A Girl's Guide to the Good Life, the quirky "style compass for the girl on the go" lifestyle had taken off—evolving from a book into a full-blown lifestyle. As one of Target's first designer collaborations, the brand expanded into furniture, bedding, and kitchenware, all infused with Cynthia's signature blend of charm, color, and unapologetic femininity. I bought into it all.

Going to the store event with my dearest friend Audrey—a fashion fanatic who color-coordinated her looks with Louboutins thanks to a job with the famed footwear virtuoso—felt like stepping back into my Chicago days. Like visiting an old friend. I spied several celebs like Philip Seymour Hoffman and Candace Bushnell in the corner and Cynthia's art gallery beau near the counter, but not the spritely designer herself. That is, until I ran right into her. Rowley's high-wattage smile beamed even brighter as she took in my map-printed pants (circa her 1995 collection) and exclaimed, "Vintage CR! You look great!" I was smitten.

Those Cynthia Rowley "map" pants had brought me luck in love on more than one occasion. With the layout of Miami being centrally located in the crotch, I had heard strange, unfamiliar boys in bars say, "Hey, I've been there." My catchphrase rebuttal? "No, I don't think you have." If the boy was super cute however, I said it with a smirk sprinkled with some "maybe you can get there" flirtation. But I wore those pants more for my love of all things Cynthia Rowley than getting male attention. Until we shook hands in the East Hampton store, I only knew of her effervescent persona from runway shows and articles that depicted her as the personification of SanDeE* from the cult 1991 movie *L.A. Story*: funny, spirited, lovable. Traits, I so wanted. Traits, I knew I had, but that I closeted. Me—with my OCD minimalist angst and career goals-mindset—took life a little too seriously. Even when my pants screamed otherwise. The irony of wearing the map pants that day was that I'd lost my own sense of direction. I was burnt out from seventy-hour workweeks trying to convince women to love themselves while building a beauty brand— and quietly anxious about the slow drift in my relationship. What AJ and I had chalked up to stress and travel was starting to feel like something harder to ignore. My meet-cute with Cynthia that afternoon was just the jolt I needed.

"YOU'VE BEEN REPLACED," I later told AJ in jest as my girl crush engulfed me. There was so much truth to this, as I had not felt this impassioned in months. Within days of the event, I reached out to Cynthia Rowley's studio in hopes of finding a way to work together on the blossoming Swell business. Since leaving the East Hampton store, I'd learned that her monthly *Glamour* column heralded a second book. *Home Swell Home: Designing Your Dream Pad* was being released and Target would launch a Swell Home Collection. I got the interview.

Showing up to an interview in the brand head-to-toe would be gauche and fawning, so I opted for windowpane cigarette pants from her mid-'90s collection paired with a white men's shirt. The look felt like the perfect marriage of my minimalism with her charming brand. The pièce de résistance was her coordinating windowpane silk scarf. I shied away from tying it around a low-slung ponytail—that felt too prim, too Jackie O. for the occasion—so I left my curls wild. At the last minute, I wrapped the scarf around my fake Prada nylon bag (a Canal Street buy I didn't feel great about, but I was eager to have the "it" bag before Mayor Bloomberg's counterfeit crackdown). The look was borrowed from the fashion icon, former *Vogue* editor, and rumored Holly Golightly muse, Babe Paley. AJ wished me well. He meant it, or tried to, but he was buried in his own job search stress and a growing panic about his uncertain future. I cared about his worries but just couldn't console him that day. I was flying too high.

Stepping off the elevator into the Cynthia Rowley studio, I entered a white walled warehouse with oversized windows and garment racks lining the perimeter. The space buzzed with action: they were prepping for a sample sale. I paused to soak in what may be my one chance for a fashion job, the drive for moving to New York in the first place. Manifesting may not have hit the zeitgeist yet, but that is exactly what I did. Smoothing my sweaty palms over my thighs and steadying myself, I focused on the Skittles-hued array of fashion. I may not have always loved the skin I was in, despite the eradication of frown lines, but I knew I was dressed for success. More importantly, I hoped what I was wearing would ultimately give way to what I promised that I could bring to the brand, given my marketing experience.

The next hour felt like a too many glasses of Champagne blackout. I have flashbacks of sitting at the oversized conference table across from the creative duo who finished each other's sentences and giggled about the success of Swell. And from Cynthia, I felt an adoring gaze, like the one AJ once bestowed on me, as we laughed over my encyclopedic recall of her designs from the past decade. While there was no job offer that day, I walked away with an assignment. I provided writing samples, ad agency recommendations, ideas for expanding the Swell brand and copy suggestions for the Swell sunglasses case. And then I patiently waited. And waited.

As the temperatures cooled, so did my relationship. While I'd been embraced at Passover, by Yom Kippur it was clear AJ's family preferred his partner be a member of the tribe. His initial open-hearted philosophy about religion shifted into a more rigid need. And the once-playful intellect that attracted me to him had hardened with unemployment. Our dates began to feel less about love and more like an SAT prep course. Over sushi one night, he chided me about reading *Women's Wear Daily* instead of *The Wall Street Journal*. "Quick, who's the mayor?" he asked half-joking. I'm no Mensa candidate, but it didn't take a genius to know he was pushing me away; career upheaval had changed him. Where our differences once made things interesting, they now made us feel incompatible. Fun frocks that had been in rotation all year were pushed to the back of the closet again as we both spent less time—and less energy—focused on each other. The poet Virgil may have said, "Love conquers all" but he didn't know the trappings of modern love in New York City. I had to face the truth: we were never going to have the kind of deeper emotional connection that makes a lovemark—much less a marriage.

Weeks later, just before Halloween, AJ left for a weekend wedding. No plus-one invited, he muttered unconvincingly. I was surprised but also relieved. I needed space. Maybe forever, I surmised—but never uttered. That Saturday morning, I rose with the sun, lingering outside Enterprise Rent-A-Car clutching my Venti Starbucks. I needed this. I had to face fears. I had no idea how afraid (and how sheltered) I had become in my relationship. Wearing navy Nike running shorts and an old college T-shirt and clutching the MapQuest printout for the eighty-minute drive to Sussex, N.J., I hopped in my rental car and sang distractedly to Barry Manilow on the radio. Traffic was light, but my heart was heavy. I knew it was time to take a leap in life.

Literally. Three hours later, I careened from 14,000 feet while attached to an enthusiastic guy. Freefalling while jumping out of an airplane, in a standard-issue prison jumpsuit—not the stylish garments they've become today thanks to Rivet Utility and my own well-worn Alex Mill—that flapped loudly in the wind was both freeing and frightening. While my tandem partner filmed us going down, I tried not to vomit. I shouted curse words. It was excruciating but I needed to take that courageous leap to remind myself that I am more than what others see and assume. Far greater than I was being conditioned to believe. This kind of confidence could not come from an injection, boyfriend or beauty slogan.

Thud. I landed hard on the ground. A stifled laugh came out with a gulp, knowing I survived the jump. But who was I kidding? I was pushed out of that plane. I had no idea if naturalist John Burroughs was right in the 1880s when he first wrote, "Leap and the net will appear." Yes, there was a parachute, but I would like to say it was me who caught myself that day. I flew then so that I could now soar.

Before landing as I had been trained—heels first, sliding into a seated position with legs stretched out like a baby doll—my eyes filled with tears. I did not need (or want) the adrenaline rush of this jump ever again, but it was clear I did need more support and connection. Much like jumping out of the airplane, life can be done alone but it's so much better (and far more satisfying) knowing there is someone attached to you. In this case, it was the parachute cord to pull. But in life, it would be a hand to hold. I stripped off the damp jumpsuit and drove over the speed limit back to Manhattan. I didn't need to "Ask Jeeves"—a quaint precursor to Google—questions about breakups. I knew what I needed to do. Like a well-worn sweater that I had donated to Housing Works, AJ needed to belong to someone else.

The breakup was swift. Not *Sex and the City* Post-it note swift, but over the phone and within seconds of our greeting. He blurted, "I just can't do this anymore..." before I even finished clearing my throat. As much as I knew it was the right decision, I fell apart. A tradition of Judaism that I understood and still revere is the opportunity to mourn, to truly commune with feelings when there is a loss, by sitting shiva. While there isn't an official shiva period for a breakup, the tradition of grieving for seven days can help with the healing process. I leaned into it.

While I never landed the role with Cynthia Rowley, despite a year and a half of staying in touch as the Swell brand expanded even further, the proximity to such a promising opportunity inspired me to explore new jobs. I just *had* to work in fashion. And my adoration for Cynthia Rowley never waned. For summers following, my beach share was mere houses away from hers, right across from Montauk's infamous surf beach Ditch Plains. I'd spend hours watching the waves to catch glimpses of her surfing, riding high with husband and kids in tow. In one of her bright, colorful rashguards, of course. To this day, she remains a reminder to dive into life and tread fearlessly.

SEVEN

Preparing America in Prada Flats

IN THE EARLY 2000s, transformation became a cultural obsession, and the beauty industry was booming. It was the era of airbrushing, reality makeover shows, and the rise of the "before and after." Beneath the glossy perfection, however, was a growing epidemic of body dissatisfaction, low self-esteem and anxiety, amplified by the lingering unease of post-9/11 life. Amid national grief and uncertainty, women turned to small luxuries—lipsticks, lotions, self-tanners—for a fleeting sense of control. Leonard Lauder dubbed it "the lipstick index." I wasn't just watching it unfold; I was helping drive it, having left Saatchi & Saatchi for a grander title and a bigger paycheck in a job to lead a portfolio of brands eager to sell confidence in a bottle.

My eyes may have been on the prize—a job in fashion—but rent was due, and beauty beckoned. I'd traded my Olay assignment for the opportunity to manage multiple beauty brands: Biore, which my younger pore-strip-obsessed self would have loved; John Frieda, who was striving to make America blond again; and Jergens, a mass market go-to moisturizer now self-tanning every limb in the country. I was firmly—oh yes, firming cream was newsworthy that year with claims to tone skin in two weeks—ensconced in work but still nursing the breakup blues. I missed having someone to text, to vent to, to say goodnight next to. Life was a whirlwind of deadlines, beauty claims, and personal heartache.

Strategic planning for the brands played to my strengths—curiosity, creativity and critical thinking—but what brought me even greater joy in my new role were the photo shoots. Specifically, and not surprisingly, the wardrobe. John Frieda's twin daughters were often the fashion-forward (and label-obsessed) models. While they loved playing dress up on camera, many of the barely worn or untouched, discarded clothes were brought back to the ad agency, unreturnable to stores. As a vice president, I strived to set an example and not be the first to pillage. Trust me, it was hard to hold back. However, when a pair of black Christian Dior moto pants—designed by John Galliano, no less—appeared outside my office, it felt like fate. After my recent loss, I just couldn't turn away from an object of my affection. Worn on rotation with starched white men's shirts and red Saucony Jazz sneakers, they fashioned a fresh start for my wounded self. I didn't need to saunter past AJ, but the Dior acquisition taught me the meaning of "revenge dressing," a term coined the previous decade thanks to Princess Di.

The fact that I still own those Dior pants makes me beam with pride. I was never a spendthrift, ever responsible—even with freebies. I believed I was neither high- nor low-maintenance. I was "no maintenance." Just a girl wading through life, chasing goals and stumbling through emotions. What I wore, which had always been instrumental in shaping who I was, was proving to have the Midas touch in resolving even emotional upheaval. And I don't even like gold.

While the Dior piece provided a boost, my doldrums were not completely erased. I considered becoming a brunette; this blonde was not having more fun. And though I usually stuck to a muted palette, I found myself reaching for something with a little more flash. When I joined friends for cocktails or a party, I turned to "going out tops," the democratic early aughts fashion staple that showed up on every sidewalk and red carpet. Embellished blouses, halters and silky tanks in colors I usually avoided suddenly made their way into rotation.

Uncoupling had erased most of my weekend plans, so I often found myself wandering through Central Park from the west side to Fifth Avenue to scour the beauty departments of my favorite stores. Even though I was staving off isolation, I chalked it up to "work research." While Barneys was notorious at the time for its beauty offerings, Bendel's rivaled the chic outpost with curated selections and an eye for start-up brands. It became known as an "incubator" for emerging and niche lines like Tarte Cosmetics, Awake, Too Faced and Paula Dorf.

One stunning, sunny day, just before heading into Bendel's, I gazed into the Prada storefront windows. Prada may have hit the zeitgeist with its tiny backpack in 1984, but it was the ugly chic of the mid-'90s that cemented its place in *Vogue* and among the fashion crowd. The breakout 1996 collection—titled "Banal Eccentricities"—was characterized by fashion press as "stiff and unflattering" with pieces in murky brown and green hues that "hovered somewhere between shades of slime and mold." Formica table graphics, librarian length skirts, and clunky T-bar sandals that were "unorthodoxly low-heeled" rounded out the looks. Critics were initially shocked, but the collection caused a sartorial shift, challenging conventional beauty and making space for intellectual style to be seen as fashionable.

Me? I loved Miuccia Prada's approach of unconventional designs, her willingness to reject traditional beauty standards in favor of something more layered, more complex. Like us. If only we could all reject beauty standards so freely, I thought then—and still do. Prada's defiance stood in stark contrast to the filtered, flawless fantasy I'd been selling—and chasing. Like 177,000 others in 2001, I'd gone under the knife to reshape my strong, Italian nose—one, not unlike Miuccia's—that was too overpowering for my face. I was a perfectionist, sure, but the retouching of models that had taken over magazines in the past decade wasn't helping my cause. Rhinoplasty felt like the only solution even though I knew unrealistic beauty can tear you down. Fashion, on the other hand—and identifying my personal style—felt like power.

Prada's current 2003 season had such a '60s vibe, with its bead embellished tops and handbags, bold solids and a black and white campaign featuring some of my favorite faces: the all-American Missy Rayder and Russian newcomer Natalia Vodianova. The shoes were breathtaking. Shiny, metallic silver open-toed flats made the perfect antidote to the ubiquitous flatform shoes sold by everyone from Chanel to Steve Madden. I gulped hard, trying not to think about my checking account's minimum balance requirement, then opened the door. I made a beeline for the silver sandals, uttering to the lithe suited man, "I should be receiving 'galimony' to pay for this." Blank stare. The silence was louder than the price tag.

"You know, financial support post-breakup," I added, before laughing a little too loudly.

"I think that's called palimony," said a woman next to me. "But that's not recognized in New York," she divulged. Living in the city with the highest concentration of lawyers in the United States, I never doubted she was right.

"Do they fit?" my Prada pusher inquired. Yes, they fit. The shoes that I would need to be buried in, given the expense, fit me perfectly. The size seven sparklers were just the thing I needed to ignite my life. The fact that I could not afford the gleaming Prada shoes—but could easily pay them off, I would convince myself, as I laid out my credit card—did not faze me. I was too overwhelmed with instant gratification. Having watched five seasons of *Sex and the City*, it felt less reckless than ever to splurge on shoes. Plus, I assured myself, you can't put a price on standing a little taller—especially in flats. Decades later, I listened to famed celebrity stylist Karla Welch's MasterClass on "Building and Owning Your Personal Style." In it, she spoke about, "the power clothing gives you to feel great about yourself." Now I know that's what came over me that day.

The reflective flats may have appeared to most as only a pair of shoes, but to me, they were so much more. Maybe it was all a mirage, but they represented a luminous future. I strolled out of the store clad in my new Prada sandals, just as I once did as a child —even though the clerk didn't bend down to hand me a lollypop and ask, "Do you want to wear these out?" I was still walking on clouds in my shiny shoes the following week when my agency merged with a larger one. My job was in jeopardy. Despite the high of new shoes, when a male British creative director said I could work on a new assignment if I'd be "comfortable promoting tampons that required women to touch themselves", I knew it was time to walk away.

It wasn't just his question—it was everything. I was exhausted: from the heartbreak, from pushing unattainable beauty, from pretending the world hadn't changed. In a post-9/11 city still cloaked in grief and fear, crafting strategies and advertising for firming creams and self-tanners suddenly felt small. And futile. I turned down the offer and walked away from a thriving career—with no clear plan for what came next.

Stepping away from beauty would leave a noticeable gap in my resume, but it made space for something that felt more mean-ingful: a pro bono role on a post-9/11 public preparedness campaign. A friend from the ad agency connected me with the prominent lawyer, journalist and entrepreneur who founded *American Lawyer* magazine and the Court TV network Steven Brill, who was spearheading a national effort to help Americans be better prepared for whatever might come next. It didn't pay, not really—just a stipend that barely covered my Starbucks habit—but it gave me something I hadn't felt in a while: purpose.

TWO YEARS after that devastating morning, New York was still grieving. The loss of 2,606 lives in the city alone had left us frac-tured, grieving and fearful. (In total, 2,976 people died that day.) What's worse: seventy-five percent of Americans admitted they wouldn't know what to do in the face of another terrorist attack. I certainly didn't have any answers. Even the fashion world, forever tied to the timing of the attacks (Liz Lange was in the middle of her New York Fashion Week runway show when the 9/11 attacks began) felt the shift. That September, many designers paused or canceled shows. In the years that followed, runways paid tribute with moments of restraint, reflection or sometimes overt patriotism—and fashion that leaned toward comfort and stability.

Brill had an idea. In 2003, he launched the America Prepared Campaign. The campaign's goal was simple but urgent: help Americans build a plan, prepare a Ready Kit, and feel more in control if disaster struck again. At that time, I was single, in my fourth year of New York life, and out of job prospects. I didn't feel great about myself. The smell and ash had finally lifted from the city, but the hard-won lesson remained: we needed to live boldly and take risks. I'd come to Manhattan to work in fashion, but in that moment, I chose to help.

Determining what to wear when meeting the successful multi-hyphenate was not an issue. A suit. All black. Having a resume the serious scholar might side-eye, as if I had been Barbie's makeup artist, I needed to show up looking professional and speak to being a brilliant strategic marketer for his endeavor. I wanted to help while I looked for a real, paying job, even though it likely meant dipping into my hard-earned 401(k). Surrounded by his close-knit team of an intern from Yale (Brill's alma mater) and a go-getter entrepreneurial shark who only paused to eat an avocado for lunch, I felt like a loser in great lip-gloss during the interview, but I was hired.

While I embarked on this compassion project, I felt more like a charity case. Within days of accepting the role, my high-strung suit gave way to the informal office wear of khakis, tees and other shapeless New England garb. When Brill was present, I leaned on tailored Theory trousers with plain tees and a jean jacket. Donning anything more comfortable would have felt too sloppy, as if I were not serious or smart enough to contribute. My silver

Prada flats made an appearance as often as I could pull them off; they continued to buoy my spirits while I spent weekends revamping my resume and chasing fashion leads through friends.

The work on the campaign was important, but about as uplifting as the Midtown office's sad beige carpet. But it mattered. Buoyed by his relentless ambition, Brill launched the "America Prepared Campaign" on the heels of his book *After: The Rebuilding and Defending of America in the September 12 Era* while simultaneously creating "Verified Identity Pass" (which later became Clear) as a security solution for airports post 9/11. His gusto and ingenuity brought my own self-pity to a halt. Life outside of the mission—my breakup and career woes—took a backseat to developing and executing with precision the commercials and marketing materials to educate the country. I repeated details of the steps ("Make A Plan", "Build A Kit") more often than my own name. For months. The office was a revolving door of notoriety including the Secretary of Homeland Security, Tom Ridge.

By the end of the assignment, more than six long months later, my work attire slid into what we now call "athleisure". Despite the term for activewear first being used in 1979, the style didn't take over for another few years when Lululemon became a household name. I donned Nike sweatpants that were easily elevated by J. Crew sweaters and button-downs. For our final task on a warm autumn Saturday, I stepped out in what had become my uniform: a pressed white men's shirt with sleeves rolled-up, navy J. Crew flat-front shorts, and my ever-loyal silver Prada shoes. I felt polished and comfortable, but not too conspicuous for my eight-hour shift at Walmart. In the heart of New Jersey, I was positioned at the front of the store amidst store employees in blue vests, greeting customers and steering them to buy Ready Kits for $25 (for one person) to $66 (for family of four size). It was an arduous, albeit rewarding, day. And the perfect way to punctuate my patriotic act and devotion to the campaign. I got a lot of compliments ("Wow, now those are some sparkly shoes!")—and comments—about my shoes.

Sure, I didn't edge any closer to a fashion job during my stint with the campaign. I had no idea of my next move when I finished out my last week with Brill and his team. As of Monday, I was unemployed again. But I did have a Ready Kit (actually, five of them) and felt oddly stronger in my conviction about my career path. Someone once said on the campaign: "In dark times, we often go inward, covering up and disguising who we are." I never forgot that. Whether it was the shiny new shoes that could not be subdued, or my newfound self-assurance that I could do anything I set my mind to, I was no longer cloaked by heartache and self-doubt. Educating the country and selling Ready Kits had been the right career risk. And while Brill's risk management ethos was top of mind, I determined I needed to put myself out there even further. In dating. With writing. As an aspiring fashion executive. I was, after all, prepared for *anything*.

While airbrushing and beauty sold in a bottle weren't going away—if anything, they would only intensify in the years that followed with filters and face-tuning apps—I knew I'd return to beauty and fashion someday. But I'd bring with me a new perspective having experienced beauty rooted in purpose. Showing up for others. Making an impact in the community. My inner beauty was shining—just like my Prada shoes.

EIGHT

Starving in Marc Jacobs Skinny Jeans

IN 1986, *Newsweek* proclaimed in a cover story that single women over forty were "more likely to be killed by terrorism than to marry," based on findings from a Yale-Harvard study. The alarming news prompted a nationwide crisis. Until the Twin Towers fell five years later. Suddenly, our fears became real.

As a Manhattanite living through the 9/11 tragedy, I watched dating do a 180. I know it sounds insensitive, but it was a legitimate response to shock and fear. Overwhelmed with fear and a myriad of questions—Will we go to war? Will we get attacked again?—people sought connection and embraced comfort in one another. For the first time, it felt like riding the subway was not about avoiding someone's Degree-infused armpit or dismissing glances, but an opportunity to engage with people. Making eye contact made you feel less alone, if only until the next stop.

I fell in love with dating during this post-apocalyptic heyday. Otherwise-commitment-phobes and Peter Pan boys wanted to meet for coffee, drinks, movies, and walks in Central Park. There were no love matches, but I made plenty of sweet memories while learning about business and life from a driven lawyer ("only do what you love for a living"), an entrepreneur about to make it big in video games ("be sure to incorporate fun in life"), and a venture capitalist who casually wore a vintage Rolex that was as beautiful as his face ("be sure to take risks"). It was like securing an MBA while staving off fear and loneliness.

There was no need to dress to impress on these dates. Clothes were relaxed; life felt too precarious to prioritize high style. You could open an envelope of anthrax any day, we'd say, so why fuss over a pencil skirt? I'd love to think my well-worn, low-rise 7 For All Mankind jeans were actually comfortable, but I suspect their familiarity brought me ease. Obsessed with Kate Moss, I'd been intrigued by a low-rise fit since the trailblazing waif strutted down the Alexander McQueen NYFW runway in "bumriders" in 1996. (In a former synagogue, no less.) Her hip bones were as prominent as her cheekbones. But let's be honest, the real credit to making this unfortunate trend widespread goes to Britney Spears.

My Sevens were slung so low, they aired out my hip bones—and I took pride in the fact that I never revealed a thong. "Thong mania" had swept the nation with its flashy, garish peek at panties, yet I held true to my minimalist style. Since the release of the Sisqó song a few years prior, the flossy undies became increasingly tackier (thanks to the rhinestone setting BeDazzler) and, like toe rings, had little purpose. Were they even underwear? Since the notorious J. Sisters—pioneers of the Brazilian bikini wax—had stripped us bare, removing every last pubic hair as you bit down on a popsicle stick to thwart pain, there was hardly anything left for the G-strings to cover. Even when celebs I adored, like America's Sweetheart Jennifer Aniston, were caught showing both the string and the ring to the paparazzi, I wouldn't waver. On rare occasions, my OCD caved to the perfectly folded Hanky Panky's sitting like fruit in a bowl next to every register, but I genuinely preferred going commando. Hey, there's nothing more minimalist than naked.

The real wardrobe shift for during this time was exchanging starched men's shirts for white "wife beaters," a term that's fallen out of fashion for good reason. While the ribbed tees, which

Hanes launched in 1928, were sold everywhere, the name was polarizing to many, including fashion editors. But I loved how the tank layered without bunching underneath a boy's department store blazer (a coup for the cropped cut and three-quarter length sleeves as much as the price) or any sweater the J.Crew catalog (its original moniker before Jenna Lyons rebranded it a "Style Guide") peddled that month. Ever since my days of working at J.Crew in Chicago, I had an affinity for their crewneck sweaters in any of the Martha Stewart-esque neutrals: ecru, almond, heather, and mushroom. I still lived in my thread worn Rollneck sweater on weekends. When Mickey Drexler took the helm in 2003, pushing aside the hunting dogs for a fashion makeover, I happily went along for the ride.

Contrary to the aspirational imagery of Elsa Klensch's CNN show, J.Crew had the uncanny ability to portray a dreamy lifestyle that *just* might be achievable. Who didn't long for a road trip with friends in an International Scout or want to cycle tandem with a beau? Given the upheaval of our lives since 9/11, nothing felt more consoling than the notion of packing it in to live upstate with someone you love to start a family. It would be a charmed life. We'd all wear tartan at the holidays. Yes, normcore dreams and attire were just what I needed to feel secure. Even my once loved "going out shirts"—silky tanks and camisoles sold everywhere from Theory to H&M (which had arrived the previous year with much fanfare)—got relegated to the back of the closet until further notice.

Regrettably, by the time Lower Manhattan Development Corporation awarded the design for rebuilding at Ground Zero in early 2003, we had relapsed. People wittingly brushed by each other again, never looking up from their phones. Hurrying to work. Scurrying to the gym. Eschewing relationships. Believing I had no choice, I began online dating. I cherished my indepen-dence and solitude but felt lonely. There are only so many ways to reorganize an 800-square- foot apartment on a Friday night. I longed to share my life with someone again. But not just anyone; I

wasn't desperate. I knew online dating was far from sexy, but its
loser stigma was dwindling.

With so many new people online, it was even slightly less
taboo. I'd never bring it up in morning meetings at my ad agency,
but I did not shy away from digital matchmaking in conversation
with friends. In the year I put myself out there like a mail order
bride, ten million more people started online dating and quarterly
revenues for popular sites were up $90 million. Revenues them-
selves are a bore, but even I knew they translated to better odds
for finding someone interesting and single—versus the stereotyp-
ical married guy trolling for sex. Or phishing for money. Bumble
founder Whitney Wolfe Herd was barely out of diapers, yet her
idea of empowering women to take charge of their online dating
spoke to me.

Right away, I called the shots by rejecting stereotypes. I'd had
enough of that with my last boyfriend, AJ. Religion, for starters.
There was no fine print keeping me, a blonde Christian, from
joining JDate, the premier online dating site for Jewish singles.
What I lacked in lingo (Reform, Conservative, Orthodox were all
similar, right?), I felt I could learn on the fly. I'd been schooled
enough by my neighborhood, the Upper West Side and home of
Zabars, Jerry Seinfeld and every Jewish boy who'd chatted me up
in bars for years, to navigate the site initially. I figured Wikipedia
could explain the rest. I took pride in my impartiality. Our
country was in crisis, after all, fighting Osama bin Laden's
expanding holy war. We'd suffered significant loss and were still
reeling from the attacks. No one could take our freedom to
choose who to love.

On JDate, I was a popular conquest at first. Most boys were
intrigued by my fair Nordic look; a few were annoyed that I was
not dating within the site's boundaries. It's okay to color outside
the lines, I wanted to retort, but never did. One lovely man asked
me to lunch and over the course of the Middle Eastern buffet, he
told me how funny and charming it was that I'd ventured onto
the site. He graciously didn't quiz me about Judaism but also

admitted he was not really a practicing Jew. "Like Jewish atheism?" I asked, grateful I'd brushed up on my notes before meeting. He smiled. I could barely hear his reply though, instead channeling my energies to determine if he had a muffin top. From one angle at the beef vindaloo station, he looked a little chubby but still very cute. By the lamb kabobs, I realized his blouson shirt was positioned just so for a reason. Spanx had not been invented for men yet.

BEING weight conscious was nothing new for me. Food was top of mind—and conversation—in my house growing up. As I was turning nine, my heavyset sister Jennifer was put on the Scarsdale Diet by our very lean mother, who had been heavy at that same age. My mom knew the heartache and cruelty of middle school. Those years are already about angst, she'd said to us, but it should not be because you weigh as much as your own father.

My mother's mindset was definitely inherited. Her generation had experienced a significant shift—almost a brainwashing—in beauty ideals. The voluptuous hourglass figure of the 1950s, epitomized by Marilyn Monroe, gave way in the 1960s, during her late teens, to a thin ideal popularized by Twiggy and fueled by the booming weight-loss industry, including the launch of Weight Watchers. Married just before turning twenty-two and settling into the role of a stay-at-home mom, my mother felt the mounting pressure to conform to these narrow standards. Diet products like Dexatrim only deepened the cultural obsession with thinness. She passed these conditioned beliefs on to me and my two older sisters, shaping how we saw ourselves and how we approached fashion from a young age. These values were also reinforced by the fashion magazines we eagerly devoured.

While G's headshot on JDate was genuine, unlike guys who displayed thirst traps of Ben Affleck or a big fish they'd caught, I felt duped. I enjoyed our easy banter and wanted to have an open mind, despite my initial lack of attraction to his less than eight-pack. He was interesting, well read and a true journalist. Having chosen the softer, creative side of journalism with my advertising career, I saw an opportunity to understand how the well-written half lived. If I had learned anything from 9/11, it was that life is unpredictable and connections with people matter. In retrospect, I realize there was something comforting in his round belly and freshly combed 1950s clean cut hair, thinning ever slightly in the back. G faintly resembled my late father, who had passed away suddenly a few years earlier. I must have felt a subconscious paternal longing as I put my number into his phone. Life in New York still felt uncertain and isolating. Why not go out on a second date?

While my father never worried about his "dad bod," I came of age watching my mom perpetually count calories, drink Tab and attend Weight Watchers when she wanted to knock off a few pounds. I thought it was customary for women to fret over the scale each morning. Weighing—then reweighing—before and after going to the bathroom. By age nine, I'd memorized calories in everything from bananas and milk to dry toast, using the Dr. Scarsdale book as a resource. By the time I met G twenty-five years later, my prowess for calorie calculation was fierce. Before he took a bite, I knew his meal's tally. Over the course of a month, and as many meals as dates, it was not his love for food that concerned me but his poor eating habits. There were not enough Tums on the planet to heal my sour stomach following our constant all-you-can-eat outings.

My fun Sigerson Morrison pointed-toe kitten heels were lost on him. I would have been better off with a pair of Nikes to jog home. At least I could have run off some of the heavy meals I ingested. After each gluttonous date, I'd shimmy into my Marc by Marc Jacobs skinny jeans to make sure I wasn't ballooning. Skinny jeans, like my foray into online dating, were newly back on the fashion scene. The arbiter of cool, Marc Jacobs, had deemed them chic. I didn't need to see his top spot on *The Face* magazine's 2003 list of the "100 Most Powerful People in Fashion"—the Standard

& Poor's index of cool—to know he was the one to wear. He'd been spearheading design for Louis Vuitton since 1997. However, he also looked out for girls like me—who loved fashion but could not afford luxury—by launching his secondary namesake line in 2001.

According to *Vogue*, the Marc by Marc Jacobs line did not revolutionize shapes or cuts but the distinction "is in the way he puts it together, as though channeling the wardrobe whims of an imaginary girl whose moods, and outfits, shift from moment to moment." With so little control in my life and the somber mood of the city, I craved the brand's whimsy and creativity. *Vogue* went on to describe the designer's vision in a way that particularly appealed to me with, "Marc is not about debutantes, punk princesses or cheerleaders, but about cool girls who follow their own rules." As the proud owner of several MBMJ pieces, which I wore habitually, I concurred. Still discovering who I was and where my life was heading, I sought freedom of expression more than ever.

Marc Jacobs had taken over Bleeker Street with six boutiques packed into just four blocks. The street was known for its lines— tourists queued at Magnolia Bakery for cupcakes, especially after *Sex and the City* featured Carrie and Miranda indulging there in season three, but the fashion crowd came for Marc. Visiting one of his boutiques was a defining part of the brand experience for me. Each store was designed by Stephan Jaklitsch, the architect behind all of Marc Jacob's retail spaces (and later, the home of his business partner, Robert Duffy). The interiors were über-chic: navy blue concrete floors, blue metal shelves stacked with perfectly folded sweaters I wanted in my own closet immediately and industrial-style suspended handrails showcasing longer garments. The music—current alternative and rock, from Sonic Youth to The Clash—played at just the right volume to set a mood without competing for attention. One evening, while browsing the store, I tried not to stare as Cameron Diaz giggled beside the handrails. Her laughter was as infectious in person as on screen.

DATING a foodie like G was challenging as I still hadn't fully reconciled how to dress a body that did not mirror my ideal. In the Midwest, I had a perfectly fine physique, even as body dysmorphia taunted me into watching what I ate; In New York, I felt chunky next to the gazelles I shopped alongside in Soho—and it didn't help to sit at Pastis beside women glaring at their food. While I ordered the approximately 1,000-calorie moules frites bathed in Pernod (See, G, I am *not* afraid of food!), they lit cigarette after cigarette. And no, not everyone was thin. But every woman I found enticing, and the men around me ogled, had jutting hip bones. That should come as no surprise, given my fixation with Kate Moss.

This obsession brought to mind a beautiful, yet bigger, girl in my advertising agency who was not only deemed unattractive but often quietly mocked for her rightful confidence. As if she didn't deserve to be above a size eight and feel good about herself. I wish I could say that the collective male gaze—and scorn—didn't impact my own self-worth. But truthfully, I saw clearly what would happen to me at work if I jumped a few dress sizes. It was sexist as hell, but I wasn't confident enough to fight it. What about her beautiful face? I wondered. It hurt to realize how little that counted. So, it was skinny jeans on rotation.

I also began filling in my formerly purged closet with minimalist designers that reflected my evolving creative identity while rendering me thin: forgiving dresses from Mayle (the designer daughter of the author Peter Mayle, whom I loved) on Elizabeth Street; edgy low-slung trousers from Daryl K, and the simplest accessories from cocktail rings to scarves from the Chelsea flea market. (Thrift shopping was key since there was only so much credit card debt I was willing to accrue, after all.) I felt like myself in these garments; my body started to feel worthy of fashion. I also realized that minimalism, with its pared-back looks, is just choosing simplicity over standing out. Aside from some singular pieces, like the infamous Trina Turk khakis and select Cynthia Rowley printed pants, I'd worked to blend in for so long. If I really wanted a big life, I had to start taking up room. I needed to learn how to shine. Within the confines of minimalism, of course. I hadn't worn a sequin since my 1976 ballet recital and was not about to revert back to my jeté days anytime soon.

G, on the other hand, happily blended into the sidewalks of New York in a casual Friday look he wore day in, day out. But he was not without his own vanity. Fluent in Portuguese, well-traveled and experienced in exploring other cultures, he proudly made each date an adventure. I quickly learned these escapades were all culinary. We explored new neighborhoods and the boroughs for Peruvian food, Rodízio (an all-you-can-eat style of Brazilian restaurant), and a churrascaria Brazilian steakhouse which featured interesting flavors and sauces. But where G saw a delicious, marbled flank steak, I saw congealed fat. There were more overzealous portions of meat and potatoes with G than I saw in my eight years living in the Midwest. When I suggested seeing bands or meeting for a drink, he would steer us to dinner and dessert outings. Had he never simply strolled through Central Park with a girl, I wondered aloud one night? Even harder to swallow was his ever-expanding waistband as he grew comfortable with me. He began apologizing for the sleep apnea and erectile dysfunction, which I am certain were tied to his burgeoning weight.

Watching G expand harkened back to memories of my sister, who gained weight in the years following my parent's divorce. She used food to bury her emotions beneath boxes of Little Debbie snack cakes. We'd find empty dishes and wrappers under her bed. Angry and bloated, her ankles buckled every time she wore her Mia clogs. I was too young to understand how much pain she was carrying; I just knew I was terrified of a similar fate and became laser-focused on food as a kid. I was the only fourth grader who brought half of a cheese sandwich to school for lunch—and knew that it was less than 200 calories.

I knew I was going to end things with G but had a hard time with the catch and release of such a kind person after all the years of dating a-holes. But I had no choice after seeing the movie *Super Size Me* together. Watching the "fast-food gastronomy" flick was nauseating, and I nearly vomited just as Morgan Spurlock did after taking down the Double Quarter Pounder with Cheese. I felt heavy from the subject, as we exited the theater. So much so that I daydreamed about how to start a juice cleanse and wondered if I could ever be brave enough for a high colonic, the rage amongst celebs who swore by it for weight loss and health benefits despite being refuted by the American Medical Association and American College of Gastroenterology. As much as I'd have loved to be wafer-thin like the emerging style maven Olsen twins, I would never shoot warm water into myself through a disposable rectal tube. I'd rather starve. Not much for fast food before Morgan's experiment, I looked at G and vowed, "I will never eat McDonalds again." Waiting at the light, at the corner of 68th and Broadway, he smiled as he took my hand and said, with not so much as a pause, "I'd love to go get some dessert."

Clearly interfaith dating was not the cause for our demise. My issues with G's epicurean ways were more a reflection of me than of him. A natural born gourmand, G was happiest building entertainment and outings around meals. Whereas my family found it entertaining upon arriving home for holidays—before we even rummaged through each other's suitcases to see new clothes or beauty products—to weigh-in. The winner weighed the least. The prize? Bragging rights for the remainder of the visit. So, yeah, it was all me. I mean, I was still apprehensive about G's well-being, but I had to face my truth: I was no healthier sipping a Venti iced soy latte all day, then eating random takeout after 7 p.m. and calling it nutrition. I was far from wholesome. I had researched fen-phen for years and even considered taking the "miracle drug" after it was linked to heart valve damage. I was stealthily sliding into a size four at the time but wanted to stay a two. But I never caved, just as I never gave in to flushing warm water up my ass to flush out weight. Deep down, I knew I wasn't truly chasing thinness; I was trying to control the chaos of life. As much as being thin was an ideal, I would never buy into the toxic mantra Kate Moss would later make infamous: "Nothing tastes as good as skinny feels." The only colonic I would have, I decided, would be for an actual colonoscopy.

Fashion designer Mara Hoffman once said, "When you want something to change in your life, you've got to understand it comes with challenging yourself to be uncomfortable...we don't change, we don't become better, and we don't evolve on any level when we stay comfortable." As much as I wanted to fit into my skinny jeans and continue to wear low-risers that brought me comfort, I needed to change. Instead of restricting calories after breaking up with G., I committed myself to Equinox. Equinox was considered more than a gym—some called it a church, others a sanctuary, and many believed the fitness journey there led to self-discovery and maximizing one's potential. Overzealous expectations for a gym, perhaps, but this crowd was riddled with over-achieving New Yorkers.

The boxing class that became my new object of affection warranted a line, similar to Marc Jacobs' on Bleeker Street, as the instructor Violet had enviable hard abs and a soft heart. Violet taught me more than a right hook and roundhouse kicks. She shared wisdom about leaning into health and fitness to find—and learn to love—myself. And I had watched enough *Sex and the City* to know dating was futile unless I genuinely loved myself first. As Carrie Bradshaw once said, "The most exciting, challenging and significant relationship of all is the one you have with yourself. And if you can find someone to love the you you love, well, that's just fabulous."

I showed up for myself and attended Violet's class frequently, feeling stronger each time. Oh, except the day I saw supermodel Gisele. That was a tough self-love day. But I returned the next morning and wedged myself into the populous front row in order to face the mirror—and myself. I hoped to see beyond my white tank undershirt with "shiksa" written in cursive (a joke from friends) and favorite Nike running shorts, past my flaws and insecurities. And the skinny jeans. I still had questions. I still needed direction. But I was done trying to shrink.

NINE

Some Devils Wear Calvin

WHILE "NOTHING" may have come between Brooke Shields and her Calvins in the '80s, the namesake brand was near bankruptcy by 1991. Revenues didn't rebound until Kate Moss tugged down Marky Mark's low-slung Calvin undies a year later. In 2002, Klein sold his company to Phillips-Van Heusen, the country's largest shirtmaker, aiming for greater global expansion. The minimalist maestro relinquished extensive control—and his ownership title —with the sale of his legacy. I was, meanwhile, still searching for mine.

Like Calvin decades before, I was trying to climb out of my own financial collapse. Having cleaned out my closets along with my 401(k) during my year of pro bono work and unemployment, I was primed when my headhunter, Marianne, called to tell me I'd landed an interview at Calvin Klein. For a role I'd been chasing my entire career: vice president of marketing.

Going in-house at a fashion company had always been the dream—and truly my reason for moving to the city six years earlier—but it was proving challenging, despite a strong beauty marketing background, well-honed instincts for brand-building and decades spent tucked behind pages of fashion magazines. My borderline religious devotion to sample sales didn't hurt either. I *knew* brands. What I didn't know, despite continuous rejections and near-misses making the cut, was what they wanted. I had begun to wonder if my age, thirty-five, might be playing a role. I was expensive and set in my ways, they likely thought. They weren't wrong.

"Always the bridesmaid, never the bride," Marianne would say each time she called to let me down. If she only knew how true this was, not just in my stalled career but in my love life. I was too busy rebuilding, narrowing in on my next role while also trying to write—and get something published—to date anyone since breaking up with G. It was more than lacking mental capacity. I was just too emotionally depleted and second-guessing everything. My instincts. My choices. My goals. In the way I had outgrown much of the clothing I had brought from Chicago and upgraded my style to reflect my ambitious persona, something deeper felt off. I'd catch my reflection in the mirror and wonder who was looking back at me. I couldn't afford therapy and knew better than to get bangs, so I did the next best thing.

I strolled to Theory, just a block from my apartment on 70th and Columbus. But this time, instead of fogging up the windows with bated breath as I peered in at the covetable fall collection, I opened the oversized door and stepped inside. I immediately felt at home in the minimalist mecca with its concrete floors, slate-gray walls, and immaculately folded merchandise arranged on handcrafted hickory tables. Everything felt calm. Deliberate. Composed. Despite all my uncertainty, I felt like I could finally exhale.

I knew I couldn't walk into Calvin the next day feeling lost. If I was going to stand a chance—at the job, at reclaiming the version of myself I'd lost during the chaos—I needed something to help pull me together. I let myself believe it was somewhere in the store; fashion never steered me wrong when it came to finding myself. In the glass storefront was exactly what I envisioned hanging in my own closet as the Calvin Klein vice president: the chic tailored neutrals and working-girl suiting separates that put

Theory on the map. I pulled a camel-colored pencil skirt from the rack. The fabric was a beautiful wool—seasonless, with just the right amount of stretch. When I slipped it on, I caught myself smiling for the first time in days. The bias cut hugged where it should and skimmed over the rest. I knew it would pair perfectly with one of my countless crisp white shirts, which always made me feel grounded. And in this case, the ensemble would subtly nod to the Calvin aesthetic. Of course, I couldn't help thinking how very Carolyn Bessette Kennedy the look was.

A Theory that delivered.

The moment of truth came when I peeked at the price. It wasn't cheap, at least not for someone draining her savings week by week, but I handed over my nearly maxed-out credit card anyway. It felt like the right kind of risk. Purchasing the pencil skirt was no guarantee of future success, but it marked a decision. A quiet promise to myself: I wasn't giving up. I had to have faith I would get that job. Walking home, I thought about a quote I'd heard from famous costume designer Edith Head: "You can have anything in life you want if you dress for it." In the past, I may have trotted out this line to justify a purchase I couldn't afford but today felt different. It wasn't just about the job; it was about stepping into the possibility of who I could be.

Highly caffeinated and freshly pressed with a subtle waft of lavender from my spray starch, I took the subway post rush-hour the next morning to arrive at the Calvin Klein offices in the Garment District ten minutes early. I didn't sit down or touch anything en route. I wanted to be spotless when meeting my potential boss for the first time. As I exited the elevator onto the floor for CRK—the in-house advertising agency named after Calvin himself, a.k.a. Calvin Richard Klein—I let out an inaudible gasp. The concrete floors, crisp white walls (that I'd heard were repainted weekly), and lone orchid perched on a silver side table (was it aluminum or chrome? I didn't dare leave finger-prints to find out) reminded me of the Theory store. It was every-thing I'd imagined when I pictured the Calvin offices. I cleared my throat and stepped forward to announce myself to the lithe recep-tionist seated behind the white walled desk.

She whisked me toward my future boss' office at a brisk clip, bypassing a maze of pristine white walls and glassed-in work-spaces. As we reached the doorway, the assistant abruptly stopped. I peered in, where iconic black-and-white Bruce Weber prints leaned against the walls. Very cool. Elsewhere, I glimpsed striking ad imagery by photographers I'd later come to recognize as Patrick Demarchelier, Peter Lindbergh, Mario Sorrenti, Craig McDean and Steven Klein. It was a real Andy Sachs moment. I started to sweat. I had so much to learn.

Then, without turning fully, a woman with long shiny sheets of chestnut hair whipped around in her Design Within Reach chic black chair and said sharply, "No. Not today."

The assistant hustled me back through the white-walled wonder and jabbed the elevator down button with a manicured index finger before I could catch my breath. "I'll call you to reschedule," she said. I couldn't even begin to take personally what had transpired; the boss barely knew my name, much less my capabilities. Marianne, who I called from the sidewalk outside the building, said as much: "I promise this is not uncommon with her. I'll call you the moment you can return." By the time I got off the subway at 72nd Street, I had a message. I was to return the following day. I re-ironed my skirt, selected a fresh white shirt and tried not to chip my barely-there clean manicure: one coat of Essie "Ballet Slipper." Maybe this was a blessing in disguise? I would be far more prepared, at least emotionally, for what I faced the next day.

Again, I was postponed to my face. "I just don't have time for this!" the boss said the following day as I stood in the doorway. The assistant, who I now knew as V, looked at me with pity, and this time, I felt the tears coming. I swallowed hard and escorted myself briskly to the elevator and out the door before I'd let any emotion show.

Standing in line at Starbucks a block away for the iced sugar-free vanilla soy latte I couldn't afford but hoped would soothe my nerves, I saw Domenico Dolce and Stefano Gabbana. Was it a sign? For a moment, I considered asking if they were hiring. But even with Sicilian grandparents, my look (and interests) couldn't have been further from the bold, outrageously opulent style of their brand. There's no chance *The Official Preppy Handbook* imagery ever made it onto their mood board. I called the only woman who could understand my pain. The same woman who showed me that style was important, but faith always got you through.

"Hi, Mom."

THOUGH I'D BEEN RAISED by a devout Catholic mother, my faith wavered. And I wasn't alone. Gen Xers like me were eschewing our upbringing of organized religion. Instead, our spirituality was being shaped by L.A. celebrities like Madonna and Demi Moore, icons who inspired us to embrace a form of mysticism known as Kabbalah and don chic red bracelets. New York City took it even further, embracing therapy as a religion. Our city was called the capital of psychotherapy after all. The island of Manhattan was small at 22.4 square miles, but people here seemed unable to find themselves. The city was fueled by "hustle culture" —my generation's particular brand of workaholism—and any success achieved never felt like enough. We were never satisfied, perpetually pushing ourselves to be better, make more money, climb up the ranks. How else can you explain why you'd put up with shoebox apartments with astronomical rents? Despite being surrounded by more therapists than bodegas in my neighborhood, and thousands of places to worship scattered across the city, I was definitely among the aimless. I'd lost my father, stalled in my career, and, as much as I hated to admit it, longed for a genuine relationship.

I had to find faith again. In something. Anything. That summer, freshly showered and dressed at 8 a.m. on a Sunday, I stepped onto the empty streets of the Upper West Side, while everyone else was nursing Cyril's hangovers in the Hamptons. I headed to the one place I thought might reconcile my angst. Not a sample sale. Church. As I strolled down the aisle for the early morning service, decked out in a DVF (sample sale, naturally) printed navy wrap dress, I heard several geriatric ladies mock me. "How low is that dress?" was all I could make out clearly from their hushed gossiping. I was so embarrassed that I slunk out of Saint Stephen's Episcopal Church and into the dense humidity, my heart pounding with alienation and anger. Holding back tears, I tried to console myself with the thought that faith wasn't about fitting in or perfect dresses—it was about finding God's presence in unexpected places. I would have loved to lean on Diane von Furstenberg herself, who famously said, "The important thing is to believe in what you do. Have a big dream and take small steps." Instead, I called the one person whose faith never wavered.

"Hi Mom."

WHEN THE CALL came for my third attempted interview, I pressed the Theory skirt once again. Clearly, the cost-per-wear was already panning out. I'd second guessed what to wear—after all, isn't insanity is doing the same thing and expecting different results?—but knew I should stay true to myself. When V delivered me to the boss's doorway, this time she swiveled around with gusto and ushered me in with enthusiasm. But as we spoke, I realized she was not so much interviewing me as sizing me up. Like a bad first date. She was incredibly passionate about both the woman I would be replacing and the work itself. I knew I could overcome the cliché of the impeccably dressed, emotionally distant female boss—my interviewer was exquisite in head-to-toe Calvin Collection—a stereotype made even more famous the previous year in Lauren Weisberger's semi-fictional novel, *The Devil Wears Prada*. Though we wouldn't see Meryl Streep, Emily Blunt and Anne Hathaway bring it to life for nearly another two years, the archetype was already deeply embedded in culture.

But as I listened to my potential boss talk, I fantasized. This wasn't just about needing a paycheck; the work genuinely sounded incredible. I had agency experience, beauty knowledge— which was a perfect pairing as I'd be overseeing fragrances and, they hoped, another attempt into color cosmetics—but I lacked hands-on experience in ready-to-wear. I assured her I was a quick study. I wanted to believe I was a compelling candidate but, even now, I'm fairly certain my long, blonde hair and pencil skirt helped land me the job. I looked the part. After my year of hardship, I wasn't above it. Naturally, the first call I made after getting the offer was to my mom, who said she'd had faith in me all along.

It may sound crazy, but the hardest part of my job was getting dressed in the morning. Running into designers and well-heeled colleagues (in Calvin Klein Collection or ck Calvin Klein looks from our European and Asian licensing partners) was hard when I lacked funds for designer pieces of my own. Despite a tightly edited closet, my wardrobe felt schizophrenic, reflecting the whims and shifts in moods of a single girl mid self-discovery, rather than a self-assured woman stepping into a senior role. Even I, the minimalist since utero with a penchant for neutrals and edgy basics, had somehow amassed lots of denim (including too much low-rise that was headed for fashion exile), "going out tops," maxi skirts and (gasp) handkerchief shirts. Much of the vacation-looking wear bore the label Calypso St. Barth—which in hindsight might have become collectibles as the brand shuttered in 2017—and Tocca, which was feminine and beautiful but built for the beach, not the boardroom.

More than a business card. A milestone.

What I needed to do was grow up—and step more fully into who I was becoming. In fashion, finances and my future. But even with well over a decade of work experience, I found myself right back where I started: repeating outfits, trying to look the part. The first months were a blur of black clothes and star-struck meetings where creatives like fashion director Fabien Baron presented fragrance concepts for the brand's next hit Euphoria. But by the time fall/winter 2005 New York Fashion Week began casting, I started to feel like I belonged—not just because I was holding my own with the work, but because I now looked the part. Between borrowed pieces from the PR closet and a strategically used employee discount, I looked like a Calvin girl who wasn't trying to fit in, but was making her own mark.

It would be easy to say my biggest takeaway from my first runway show (and creative director Francisco Costa's fourth for the label) was look #16. I bought the caramel patent leather skirt with mink banding, which paired with an architectural, woven knit short-sleeved top, the moment it hit the Collection store that fall. Thanks to our thirty percent employee discount, it came in just under $800—still astronomical for me at the time—but I wore for well over a decade. It didn't just hold up, it held meaning. But the truth is, it was the energy of the show itself that stayed with me. Natalia Vodianova, the Russian beauty I often compared to Kate Moss as both were not only iconic for the brand but defining faces in fragrance, opened the show. Thanks to Baron, who brought Vodianova to Calvin Klein's attention, she became the face of Collection and our upcoming Euphoria launch.

I had watched Elsa Klensch cover runway shows for years, but nothing compared to feeling the music pulse through the room and seeing lights beam across the runway in person. The models —show ponies, really, with hair extension-length, poker-straight ponytails—strode in slim, circa-sixties silhouettes. Everything was minimalist in hue, but rich in texture: mink, shearling, cashmere, satin. I took my eyes off the runway only briefly to glimpse at the crowd: Claire Danes and Katie Holmes perched in the front row, among the fashion elite.

But the buzz of excitement fizzled like day-old Champagne at the afterparty. And, to no surprise, this event has had the longest-lasting imprint on me. While my colleagues and I took cars to Milk Studios for the show, we had to hustle back to the office afterward to wrap up work and change for the evening's festivities. I swapped my fitted black work dress for black leather shorts, a crisp white men's shirt, and signature five-inch black Calvin heels. I had just met with our jewelry licensee, so I threw on a pair of thin, oversized hoops. "Very Salt-N-Pepa," a fellow marketing vice president, Diana, said with a smile.

I walked into the after-party and was greeted from afar by a very senior executive. He waved me over, smiling with his hand outstretched. I was aghast that he recognized me so quickly and straightened my posture to make a good impression. Our "Wasn't the show spectacular?" small talk lasted only a moment. He then said, "You look great. Twirl for me." As if I were a cake topper. But I did what I was told. I smiled, pirouetted, and watched him and his ogling adult son walk away, laughing. I stood there, suddenly hyper-aware of my bare legs, my borrowed confidence. Whatever I had hoped to find at the event was no longer there for me. I left the party moments later.

The next morning, the office buzzed with Fashion Week energy, but I kept my head down. The clothes still fit, but something in me didn't. Even my fashion staple—the crisp white shirt that I usually wore like a superhero cape—hung differently now, draped in defeat. And for the first time, I considered my brusque boss differently. I would never know what, if anything, she had been through—or put up with—as one of the only women in the C-suite. It may have been the "girl boss" era, but empowerment didn't always come with safety. Or solidarity. She was polished, razor-sharp, and demanding, yet also unreadable—an enigma clad in head-to-toe Calvin Collection. What I had assumed was detachment (or, let's face it, irritation), I now suspected was her armor. She was guarded, as if she'd been asked to twirl before, too. I was just grateful that my new perspective gave me a greater confidence in her presence.

Weeks later, in a rare instance of driving together to a creative meeting in her black town car, we sat side-by-side. I stared out the window, silent, listening to the tap, tap, tap of her BlackBerry. I tried not to breathe too loudly. So maybe confident wasn't exactly where I had landed, but I felt better in her presence than I ever had. Until she touched the sleeve of my jersey dress, bought for a song at a Collection sale. "What song do you like better for the new fragrance work?" she asked.

I broke into a sweat instantly. She rarely asked my opinion, and I was both honored and terrified of giving the wrong answer. But there was something in her eyes that said I was safe. The fact that she had become the devil I knew—though with far fewer theatrics—didn't preclude me from seeing her as a woman who had fought hard to get to the top.

"I like Minnie Riperton's 'Lovin' You,'" I said. "It's perfect in the recent Bridget Jones movie." I blanked at the other options, knowing this was my favorite.

She nodded along in agreement and then, once we were in the meeting, said: "Christine loves this version, and she's really in touch with this audience."

I could be wrong, but she may have even winked at me. Then again, maybe it was just a tic. You never really knew where you stood with her—but in that moment, I felt seen. And that meant everything to me.

She left the company not long after. By the time the next Fashion Week arrived, there was a new boss—this time an angel, and someone I remain close to today. Over the years that followed, Ellen and I collaborated on some of the most challenging—yet rewarding—initiatives of my career. She believed in me early and often, offering support that made it easy to rise to the occasion. My "twirl for me" dictator had also left the company, and with his departure, I stopped fearing an elevator run in. Every day, I held my head high.

The personnel shifts felt like the end of something. And, as fashion always promises, the start of something better. I thought of Anne Klein's wise words: "Clothes aren't going to change the world. The women who wear them will." For the first time in a long time, I believed I could be one of them. Surprisingly, not because of what I wore—even though I had leaned on the Calvin clothes to find my way there—but because, finally, nothing could come between me and who I was meant to be.

TEN

Super Saturday in Tory Burch Tunics

WHILE Y2K CAUSED a global frenzy at the turn of the century, New York City was equally buzzing for a different phenomenon: the "It girl." Despite the absence of social media, these chic creatures were well-known by name and occupation (see the *Vogue* masthead). In September of 2000, *Vanity Fair* released an "It girl" list featuring heiresses—Samantha Boardman, Aerin Lauder and Kidada Jones among them—who loved to party and shop with unabandoned ferocity. The fashion world, especially in New York, took note. Park Avenue, renowned for its luxury real estate, housed many of these swans, as the line between "It girls" and socialites blurred as effortlessly as that between art and fashion. As the vice president of marketing at Calvin Klein overseeing ready-to-wear and beauty, I devoured *Vogue* writer Plum Sykes' thinly veiled tome about these society sweethearts, *Bergdorf Blondes*. The book was a fabulous read that mirrored life uptown. Or, in my case, Super Saturday.

Super Saturday, the annual Hamptons charity event *The New York Times* coined the "Rolls Royce of Garage Sales" was originally launched by Donna Karan and Liz Tilberis, the beloved former British *Vogue* editor-in-chief who resurrected *Harper's Bazaar* in 1992. When Tilberis passed away from ovarian cancer

seven years later at just fifty-one, a loyal following coalesced to
boost her legacy and the profile of the Ovarian Cancer Research
Fund by expanding the event. The shopping extravaganza now
merited ticket prices at $450 for entry, $650 if you wanted the
coveted gift bag. As I often relied on my credit card for groceries, I
just couldn't justify attending, regardless of charitable intentions.
In the summer of 2005, with a summer share in Montauk, my
dream of browsing hundreds of upscale fashion brands in a
colossal designer yard sale was realized when Calvin Klein needed
volunteers. Yes! I grabbed a white "Super Saturday" logoed white
tank undershirt, the uniform we'd wear to work at our brand
table, before anyone else had fully considered their weekend plans.

Off-duty uniform for a cause.

I was the first from the Calvin team to arrive at Nova's Ark
Project, the 95-acre sculptural park in Water Mill anointed for
Super Saturday, slathered in sunscreen and with an Olsen twin-
sized Starbucks in hand. We had a long day ahead of us and I felt
first-day-of-school giddy. Karan was milling around, along with
Kelly Ripa, Molly Sims, Nicky Hilton and Rachel Zoe, who'd
begun duplicating her '70s-inspired boho waif look for "It girls";
her latest poster child was Nicole Richie. We displayed minimal
offerings (so on brand) for sale like sleek aviator sunglasses from
our eyewear licensing partner Marchon and banded Calvin Klein
underwear, along with T-shirts in black, white and gray. (In my
mind, the only hues that mattered.) Our boxed merchandise,
lined up like soldiers on a white tablecloth, did not require try-

ons, unlike fellow fashion brands with clothing samples on rolling racks, whose wheels sunk into the dewy grass that morning. It made our booth a destination for shoppers rushing to make a purchase.

Between restocking underwear from our hidden stash beneath the table, we gave each other breaks to stroll the grounds. I was more interested in what was for sale than the celebrity petting zoo (hello Amanda Hearst and Shoshanna Lonstein Gruss)—although as a five-year *Law & Order: Special Victims Unit* fan, I stared for more than a second at Mariska Hargitay. Despite the Hamptons haute reputation for outsized cost on everything from real estate to donuts, the prices here rivaled T.J. Maxx. And the event still raised millions. While I was thrilled to browse brands I had been working into my wardrobe—Theory, Helmut Lang, Ports 1961, DVF and Rag & Bone—I knew enough from experience to hold off on purchases. Prices dropped every hour. No one, especially those who'd been toiling in the heat, wanted to return merchandise that was mauled (lipstick-stained and sunscreen smeared is not a good look) back to show-rooms. As the sun set, I felt blissful, albeit a bit greedy, walking away with more than the enviable swag bag filled with thousands of dollars' worth of beauty products. I also walked off with the majority of Tory Burch's inaugural clothing line for free. While the socially connected fashion newcomer was making a name for herself—I had DVRed her appearance on *Oprah* months prior and was in awe of her launch success, especially when the queen of daytime TV called her, "the next big thing in fashion"—she had not sold much of her collection at Super Saturday.

Burch's ladylike line of logo flats, tunics and caftans was no coincidence given her stylish upbringing in a tony section of Pennsylvania. What helped her early on was the rise of "Park Avenue princess" chic, led by Michael Kors. Polished, sophisti-cated fashion was a welcome change, given the previous decade's run of bad style borne from reality TV and L.A. influence. (Ed Hardy anyone?). I was open to experimenting with styles, but wasn't about to buy into trends in my mid-thirties. I didn't sway with the tides. I never owned a trucker hat; I was not planning to start a love affair with Lily Pulitzer-inspired looks. But I took home and categorized my windfall of the Tory Burch tunics and caftans, from demure country club prep to sparkling Studio 54 glitz, before I determined if the pieces would work within my more restrained style. If Tory Burch could venture into fashion design with no prior experience, while bearing the label "socialite," I could certainly step out of my minimalist mold and don a hot pink, sequin-embellished tunic. At least for one evening out.

Paired with white shorts, as if to offset the drama of the tunic, I headed to The Talkhouse in Amagansett. While you came for the live music—a roster of cover bands like Booga Sugar that remained obscure beyond the perimeter of Montauk Highway—you stayed (into the wee hours) for the cheap drinks and lively crowd. Despite feeling like I was dressed in a costume, I met someone. A newly minted Ironman who was more than cute, he was genuinely interesting. Worthy of a long conversation and phone numbers exchanged, which was unheard of in this dive bar, where a "serious relationship" meant knowing someone's last name. Maybe it was the shirt, the fashion equivalent of a shooting star, that made James notice me. I was unforgettable that night. I thought, *Hmm. Perhaps Tory Burch will become a go-to brand for me after all?*

I opted to wear a Super Saturday find more befitting of my style the following day when I drove James back to the city. We stopped for dinner on the water, overlooking the yachts in Sag Harbor, before departing the Hamptons. I felt comforted and confident in my new oversized pale green Theory cashmere sweater paired with my staple J.Crew white chino shorts. But the true ease came from the hours of engaging conversation during the drive. James and I quickly fell into step, spending weekends together in the Hamptons and weeknight dates as a couple in Manhattan, work permitting. The more time we shared together, the more euphoric I felt. Having just launched a Calvin Klein fragrance named Euphoria, which became the biggest brand in our scent portfolio, I knew the headiness of this word. I chalked it up to falling in love while also achieving career highs. Life could not have been better. Until, I had three seizures.

DRESSED in the only thing that felt soothing for an ER visit—a white button-down shirt, boyfriend jeans and black Converse high-tops—I let James escort me to the hospital. We spent hours there as I endured MRIs and MDs reviewed my case. Apparently, those euphoric feelings had been "auras," which are precursors to seizures. What James witnessed, in the middle of the night, were three consecutive seizures in my right frontal lobe. The epilepsy diagnosis was swift. As medication was discussed, the doctor gingerly probed our future.

"What are your plans for children?" he asked.

Whoa. We hadn't even said "I love you." I felt it, but was gun-shy. Dating in the city that never sleeps, and countless *Sex and The City* episodes, had conditioned me to hold back. Never blurt out the loaded "love" word prematurely. As our awkward pause held fast, the doctor concluded I was in prime child-bearing age—just what James needed to hear at that moment, thanks Doc. He prescribed accordingly.

My thoughts were scrambled yet my beau remained calm and composed, handling the crisis with grace. While I couldn't get former boyfriends to commit to New Year's Eve plans, James was already calling friends in medicine for advice and soothing my frazzled nerves as I grappled to regain a sense of normalcy.

Still, I grieved as if there'd been a death. *Wasn't there, I thought?* The diagnosis felt surreal–something that happened to other people, not to a healthy thirty-something fashion executive living in Manhattan who was falling in love and crushing a boxing class three times a week at Equinox. My initial confusion was replaced with overwhelming fear. I couldn't drive for a year. No cocktails either. Epileptics are *not* "It girls."

Because the seizures occurred in my right frontal lobe—the area linked to creativity—I worried about losing my intuition, imagination, emotional capacity. Would this keep me from becoming a writer? The doctor cautioned that memory may be impacted with the initial medication, an old-school epilepsy drug they leaned on as they explored longer-term options. I was so strung out by my limitations, my biggest fear didn't hit me until I returned to work several days later: would I lose my job at Calvin? I may have been physically stronger than ever (thanks, Violet), but I was emotionally fragile. I couldn't imagine James staying by my side through this.

In a bid for control and much needed comfort, I retreated to my closet. My new life called for clothes that I could count on under *any* circumstances. Now more than ever, it was time to jettison pieces that rarely left their hangers. The first items to go were the diaphanous Super Saturday boho clothes. Who was I kidding? I wasn't headed to Coachella. The colorful Tory Burch caftans and tunics had been exiled to the back as they clashed with my style, despite my attempts to be more adventurous. They reminded me of early dating days with James, but even nostalgia wasn't a good enough reason to keep them. Life felt bleak. I saw myself as damaged goods, a charity case. But delivering the neatly folded piles of bohemia to Housing Works buoyed my spirits. Usually, a visit to the thrift store brought me joy because of the impeccably styled window displays that would make Simon Doonan proud, but on that day, it was due to a sobering realization: my own diagnosis paled in comparison to the reality of people living with HIV.

The timing of my closet overhaul couldn't have been better. Beyond gaining personal perspective, the fall fashion shows declared it was time to break away bohemia. Despite front rows dotted with "It girls" in skinny jeans and peasant blouses, runways showed modern clean lines and architectural silhouettes. I hastily started incorporating Francisco Costa's architectonic looks—including the caramel patent leather skirt from an earlier collection—lean satin pants and spare, but luxurious knits. I was just beginning to find my footing when everything came to a halt. Again.

One afternoon, while presenting to Tom Murry (the CEO of Calvin Klein), I lost my train of thought. Tom, like my direct boss Ellen, was incredibly kind. They both understood this wasn't like me. I had worked there long enough to prove my capabilities, and they understood my unique circumstance. But then it happened again. And again. My memory was slipping. I stopped trusting myself and would spend extra hours in the office scrutinizing my work. I'd worked so hard to loosen my grip on perfectionism and was now clinging to it. These were more than scattered lapses in memory. They were spells that rattled my identity and shook my faith in myself. James would find me zoned out and fear I was having an aura. Was he afraid I would leave the stove on next? When doctors recommended a four-day hospital stay to explore the issue, I didn't argue.

Being hooked up to an EEG for the week called for functional fashion that also soothed my nerves. The oversized men's shirts that I once again brought to the hospital made the perfect complement to gray American Apparel sweats. (I prided myself on never buying Juicy Couture sweatpants; I could never understand the merit of advertising on my ass.) Along with familiarity, the button downs provided easy access for electrode wires to run from my scalp to my chest. The nurse helped me braid the wires into my fresh blowout before James arrived the first evening. I popped my collar for good measure, a feeble attempt to feel like myself. At that moment, my clothes felt like armor, offering a semblance of the confidence I desperately needed. You wouldn't know by looking at me, but I was terrified.

Before settling down next to my hospital bed, James smiled and handed me a book titled *It's Not About the Bike: My Journey Back to Life* by Lance Armstrong. The (pre-doping) autobiography brought me to tears. Although the only bike I rode was fixed to the floor in a spinning class, the need for inspiration is universal. James' thoughtful gesture was yet another indication that he was perfect for me. That's the thing about dating and fashion and—as I was learning the hard way—medication. With enough trial and error, you finally find what works best for you. In my case, a new medication given over the four-day stay while brain activity was monitored, helped bring my memory back to elephant status—and kept neurological issues at bay.

Over the following months, I donned my Ann Demeulemeester dress a lot. It felt like a weighted blanket and reminded me of more self-assured times. With each wearing— over black fitted Theory trousers or with Marc by Marc Jacobs skinny jeans or sans pants and paired with Calvin Klein heels—I started to regain my sense of self. By the time spring collections arrived in stores—boasting feminine silhouettes and loose, unstructured pieces in metallic hues and crisp whites—I, too, was ready to shine again.

The following year, Tory Burch not only won the CFDA award for "Accessories Designer of the Year," but she also dated Lance Armstrong. But it's the more recent "Toryssaince" that reconnected me with the brand. Nearly twenty years after launching her namesake company, the famed founder stepped fully into the design role rather than running the business. This shift brought praise from fashion media and a following from multiple generations of the latest "It girls." Burch deems the latest collections truly reflect who she is and allow us greater self-expression. I believe her recent success comes not only from great design, but also from showing women that reinvention isn't just possible —it's necessary. That we're not defined by one moment or one role, but a series of second, third (and God willing) fourth acts where we learn, grow and discover our true selves.

TORY BURCH and I have come so far since Super Saturday. We've both evolved. Neither would be caught dead in a hot pink sequin tunic now. Not because we've lost our sparkle, but because we've learned how to shine on our own terms. For me, that means living with epilepsy—taking medication every day, navigating the unknown and still showing up with purpose and grit. It may not be what constituted an "It girl" in the eyes of *Vanity Fair*, but I feel like I became one along the way.

ELEVEN

Urban Myth Manolos

ACCORDING to a study in *The Journal of Research in Personality*, our shoes—their color, condition, and heel height rather than the brand—are a personality tell-all. I wore pristine 120-milimeter Calvin Klein Collection heels daily to stride like a boss and personify employee of the year as I followed in the footsteps of legends like Carolyn Bessette, who graced the stark hallways of the designer's headquarters until she left to become Mrs. John F. Kennedy Jr. Believing in shoe maestro Manolo Blahnik's opinion that "shoes are the quickest way for women to achieve instant metamorphosis," I knew I had to stand tall.

I also learned to run in heels while working at Calvin Klein. My stamina stemmed as much from dashing between floors for meetings as it did from being a budget-conscious subway straphanger. Unlike me, the stiletto-wearing Condé Nast girls, known outside of 4 Times Square as "Condé Nasty" for their snobbery, were bestowed town cars. Their budgets were as endless as Anna Wintour's eyewear collection. Si Newhouse was more benefactor than CEO, ensuring they remained enviable with lush expense accounts, clothing allowances and mortgage loans. The "Voguettes" had their foot in the door at every restaurant, spa and fashion show but rarely walked more than fifty feet in heels.

When the media powerhouse moved downtown to One World Trade, a generous step toward rebuilding the neighborhood post 9/11, businesses flocked to the scene.

Prior to Fall Fashion Week 2005, an invite for Seventh on Sale crossed my onyx desk. I was not asked to attend the $3,000-per-head exclusive event led by Anna Wintour, but rather to work it. Despite the ten-year gap since the last gala, the mission to raise money for HIV/AIDS remained crucial given a spike in cases that year. I loved the opportunity to help the cause and, selfishly, feel like a *Vogue* staffer. Housing loan not included. Count me in.

With Calvin colleagues in tow, wearing the required uniform that mimicked my daily attire—a pressed white Ralph Lauren oxford shirt and flat front black pants—I felt at ease. The white half apron, artfully designed with the red "7th on Sale" logo, had multiple pockets to hold order pads and pens to note purchases by celebs and the evening's influential fashion crowd. Cashmere sweaters in every color for rock star spouse Trudie Styler. A Ralph Lauren jacket for socialite Tinsley Mortimer. While J.Lo's backside grazed mine, which she did not notice as she animatedly talked with her dates Domenico Dolce and Stefano Gabbana, she opted not to buy anything from my ready-to-wear section. Seeing Michael Kors sashay by with Ellen Pompeo was fantastical, thanks to my devotion to *Grey's Anatomy* as well as to the designer himself. I fell hard for talent and humor when he debuted his Spring 2000 *Palm Bitch* runway show. But the real thrill of the evening had to be meeting the queen herself—Anna Wintour—who thanked us all at the end of the evening for a job well done.

As the creative masterminds behind the event had transformed the downtown studio space into a winter wonderland from the upcoming movie *Chronicles of Narnia*, no detail was spared. Except a prompt cleanup crew. After witnessing no shortage of air kisses, we untied our aprons and shopped freely. Prices were slashed. It was a fire sale, and we were hot for merchandise we'd never be able to afford again. I draped a Dior chocolate brown crocodile trench over my shoulders, as every fashion editor is wont to do, and shouted to my Calvin colleague Diana, who was knee deep in collections of Verdura jewelry, "Too much on me?" Honestly, I knew I would buy it, no matter what she said. High from my $25,000 trench sale savings, I moved over to shoes. I was knocked off my feet when a pair of Manolo Blahnik black patent Mary Janes—called the "Campari" by the designer but better known as the "urban shoe myth" style when Carrie Bradshaw swooned over them in the *Vogue* closet seasons prior—were within reach. And in my size. (Unlike Carrie Bradshaw who said, "If these don't fit, so help me...I'm gonna wear them anyway.")

While I knew the money went to charity and people in need, I, too, felt rewarded that night. Giving back through community service always buoys my spirit, but I still wear both the Dior trench and Manolo Mary Janes with abandon today. It's been twenty years since that night, but the fashion from the evening clearly had a lasting impact on my life; transforming ensembles and my persona with each negligible cost-per-wear.

A few months later, I took the Manolo Mary Janes for a spin to the Fragrance Foundation's 34th Annual Awards (Fifis), where our best-selling fragrance Euphoria was a finalist for the Women's Luxe award. That night, my Coty client Catherine—a striking woman with a sharp eye, minimalist uniform of Jil Sander and Céline, and a taste for creative risk—was also being recognized for her work in the booming celebrity fragrance space. We can thank her for bringing J.Lo and Gwen Stefani fragrances to market. Her signature red lips made a bold statement against her chic silver crop as she took the stage to accept her award from Sarah Jessica Parker—there on behalf of her fragrance, Lovely, which was up for Best Ad Campaign. The ad, a pink-hued dream featuring SJP twirling in a tea-length gown, was overseen by Catherine herself. SJP affectionately called her "Catherine the Great," and the entire room applauded in agreement.

I was honored to be there on behalf of Calvin—and, if I'm being honest, eager to take in the crowd: a perfume-drenched mix of industry power players, celebs (I was not leaving without meeting SJP), and just enough fashion eye candy to make it worth borrowing the gown. I'd rummaged through the Calvin sample closet in between meetings earlier that week, looking for something elegant yet minimal to pair with my prized shoes. (FYI: I never cheated on Calvin and never wore my Manolos to work. You don't step on the accessories designer who dresses you.) The formal options were stunning—if snug. Very snug. Vanity sizing was in full effect at the time, as was the now-infamous introduction of size 00, thanks to Nicole Miller. As if I needed the reminder to watch my weight. I wanted to look chic, but I also wanted to breathe.

By Invitation Only.

Despite a personal allegiance to Estée Lauder's Youth Dew Amber Nude—Tom Ford's sex-driven update of the classic, launched just after his Gucci exit—I genuinely wanted Lovely to take home the gold. Seated at a table that was next to SJP's perch, I planned to sidle up, Manolos in full view, and offer my congratulations when she did win. I barely gave the iconic actress time to absorb her victory before tugging, like a toddler, on my client Lori's dress for an introduction. SJP had just sat down, taken a sip of water, and was basking in the adoration of her table. The ceremony was winding down, and I was ready. Lori, my Coty "fragrance BFF" (as James jokingly called her given how often we spoke), walked me over and made the introduction. Lori called her Sarah Jessica. I locked onto her ocean-blue eyes as she reached out to grasp my hand, warmly.

"Hello," I croaked. Then, after clearing my throat, I managed with far more enthusiasm: "Congratulations."

"Oh, thank you!" she giggled.

She was all Carrie Bradshaw to me in that moment. She glanced up toward the stage, and I knew the conversation was over but all I could think was: *Look down! Look down! I'm wearing the urban myth shoes!* It sounds needy now, but I wanted her to see—and acknowledge—that I was wearing the shoes. Our encounter was brief. She never noticed. I wasn't hoping for a friendship or a photo op—just a shared appreciation between two women who know a legendary heel when they see one. It didn't matter in the end that she didn't see my shoes. She was truly every bit the moniker of her scent: lovely.

Like a modern-day Cinderella, I returned the gown the next day. I loved the opportunity to dress up for the job, but I knew those moments were fleeting. Plus, I didn't want to get ensnared in the perks; after all, I was not Condé Nasty. The reason my Blackberry had become an appendage was clear: I was determined to be instrumental to the Calvin Klein legacy. I vowed to steer the brand toward growth and shape new products and creative. But something existential had begun to nag at me.

One afternoon, I teetered in my heels at the elevator on my way to meet Tom Murry, my kind CEO. *Is this all there is?* I thought, staring at the white walls. The glossy glory of fashion was starting to tarnish in my eyes. I realized that I was finding more meaning outside the walls of my concrete office. There was the overwhelming love I felt for my boyfriend James—even though we had yet to say those three words. What did I really want in life? A C-suite seat or a rich life that felt like mine?

I entered my CEO's office and barely sat down before he uttered, "Christine, we'd like to give you a clothing allowance."

Shit, I thought. The greater the privilege, the higher the shoes. I was already wearing the highest heels I could muster. Then again, the allowance would make for good dinner party banter even though it would never compare to the substantial finance crowd bonuses, which were the equivalent of an East Hampton house, that were often discussed.

MY DEDICATION to heels ignited both an ambassadorship to the Calvin Klein brand and a boost to my confidence, much like shoe-connoisseur Jenna Lyons who said, "I can throw on a silver five-inch heel pump and all of a sudden, I feel a little bit prettier." But more than feeling pretty, for me it was about being seen. Vertically challenged, having reached my full sixty-one inches by ninth grade, my towering heels brought me eye to eye with senior executives. Dressed the part, I felt like a force to be reckoned with; a voice worth hearing. It's no secret that heels hold power. Influential women from Sheryl Sandberg to Marissa Meyer are featured in stilettos on the covers of *Time* and *Vogue*. And prominent stiletto seller, Jimmy Choo co-founder Tamara Mellon, agrees: "Heels create a mood and psychological shift, like doing the Wonder Woman stance for confidence." No cape required.

As winter thawed and the spring collection arrived at our Madison Avenue store, I found low flats showcased in the gallery-inspired John Pawson-designed space. The shoes sat alongside '60s-reminiscent empire waist dresses in chiffon and georgette, as well as draped jersey pieces, all in signature Calvin neutrals. Despite my growing doubts about a career in fashion, I began to chip away at my clothing allowance. With a new boss on board, I felt increasingly confident, more vocal and valued at work. Still, I often found myself returning to the wisdom of legendary editor Diana Vreeland, whose influence lives on—not just in fashion history, but through her grandson, who was my ready-to-wear client. He held the license to produce Calvin's bridge line, lower priced designer apparel competing with brands like Tory Burch, DKNY and Theory. In my head, I'd replay the words of the former *Harper's Bazaar* and *Vogue* editor-in-chief: "It's not about the dress you wear, but about the life you lead in the dress."

The truth is being seen—truly seen—did not require flashy

stilettos or towering platforms. Maybe it didn't require shoes at all. One evening, barefoot in a threadbare oversized T-shirt and Calvin boy short undies, I looked up at the man I adored and thought about what Carrie Bradshaw once said: "I am someone who is looking for love. Real love. Ridiculous, inconvenient, consuming, can't-live-without-each-other love." I had found it.

"I love you," I said to James—reaching up on my tiptoes to kiss him.

TWELVE

Wild about Calvin Klein Cosmetics

BEFORE "CLEAN BEAUTY" hit the zeitgeist, chemical-laden luxury products drove the now $500 billion global makeup industry. Rich-hued lipsticks commanded $75 per tube. Packaging was ostentatious or adorned with gritty street art—and nearly every designer with a runway show had a complementary makeup line. Despite two earlier failures to monetize fresh dewy faces with branded minimalist cosmetics—first with an eighteen-piece collection in the '70s, followed by a short-lived, high-priced line under the Collection label (criticized for muted tones and lack of payoff)—Calvin Klein was optimistic the third launch would be a charm.

I embodied the brand aesthetic, thanks to hard-earned glowing skin and a penchant for a bare face save for concealer and mascara. But as vice president of marketing my role was to successfully bring this new, fashion-forward makeup line to market. Under the ck Calvin Klein label, it included the expected signature neutrals along with trend-driven seasonal shades and "splashes of intense color" like fuchsia lips and yellow lids. No pressure.

Developing the next iteration of Calvin Klein's cosmetics captured the essence of Charles Dickens' famous first line: "It was the best of times, it was the worst of times." Despite our strong partnership with a beauty licensee familiar with Calvin Klein's unique identity and vernacular, the executive team forged a collaboration with a beauty company whose greatest claim to fame was a drugstore brand riddled with glitter. A clear clash of aesthetics. The ink was barely dry on the contract when I met the new licensing partners and realized that not only did we not speak the same brand language, but we didn't speak the same language. English was, for their leadership team, a second language. Determined to overcome the communication challenges—and prove to my boss (and myself) that the recent seizure diagnosis did not debilitate me—I focused on bridging gaps between our teams, leveraging every opportunity to align visions and redefine communication strategies. For me, this was not merely about producing makeup. My mission aimed much higher. I wanted us to make a statement in the fashion industry and establish a beauty identity that would (finally) resonate and endure.

The development year was a blur of creative energy. I worked alongside creative visionaries—from Fabien Baron, the legendary art director I'd worked with on the Euphoria fragrance brand when I first joined Calvin, who'd reinvented the magazines I spent years dog-earing (*Italian Vogue* and *Harper's Bazaar*)—to famed makeup artist Mark Carrasquillo. Together, we conceived the high gloss line. The extensive collection featured 210 SKUs (stock keeping units, or individual products), focused on foundations, eye shadows, lipsticks, and lip glosses—in dramatic shades and varied textures. Powders, concealers, illuminators, blushers, eyeliners, mascaras, eye and brow pencils, lip pencils, nail lacquers and brushes completed the offering. Some of the best moments were spent working alongside PR crafting the names for shades—we'd spend hours laughing while bringing personality and narrative to the collection, ensuring each product told a story that resonated with the brand's fashion-forward, edgy identity.

It was the era of NARS "Orgasm" blush, but even with Calvin's provocative DNA, our names stayed tame. It was an ambitious number of products but spoke to the brand's commitment to shade diversity (a decade before Rhianna launched Fenty and revolutionized the category with her range) and a wide-reaching launch. The palette was designed to mirror the seasonal hues of ck Calvin Klein fashion, so I spent time with our Global Creative Director Kevin Carrigan, who taught me about the balance between designs that are functional and those that inspire. He also shared when to say "uncle" with a licensee. (He'd been with Calvin for decades and had seen it all.) One standout from the collection was Delicious Light Glistening Lip Gloss in "Glory," a sheer, brownish plum that became a favorite of Carrasquillo. "I wish all women's lips looked like that," he said. The idea behind the shade, he explained, was to make the lips look "kind of bruised, as if they've been making out all night."

While the creative vision was clear and inspiring, I had a lot to prove. I grew hoarse from negotiating the packaging. I knew women would gravitate toward a compact or lipstick tube design they'd be proud to hold—not just functionally, but emotionally. At the time, we instinctively understood what future studies would later confirm: makeup isn't just about appearance—it's tied to confidence, identity, even perceived competence. (It would be years before a Harvard study revealed that people in the workplace find women wearing makeup "more likable.")

Our campaign emphasized a connection to fashion, aiming to bridge the gap between apparel and accessories for multi-cultural, fashion- forward women. The stark white logo on solid black and over-molded transparent Lucite was stunning. Quintessential Fabien Baron. But it also cost more than the licensing partner wanted to spend. We sought compromises that wouldn't dilute the brand. Weeks were lost in debate over the doll-size applicators found in eyeshadow palettes, and other possible cost-cutting measures that could come off looking cheap or scream drugstore. I said, "This is how we do things at Calvin" in writing and on calls twenty times a day, fueled only by Starbucks iced lattes. I became so integrated with store planning that the Calvin team bestowed upon me an "APPROVED" rubber stamp for merchandising layouts. The day we got Design Within Reach's Lem Piston-designed stools, which cost almost $1,000 a pop, approved for makeup artist applications in store, I went out for a cocktail.

That night, I iced my "Blackberry thumb"—yes, a real arthritic condition—while communicating across time zones, with our team in New York, clients in Los Angeles, and the execs at the licensee's headquarters in China. I had always been an impassioned communicator and wasn't just advocating for what women wanted—I was determined to fight for Baron's vision. He understood the Calvin DNA better than anyone. But I learned a lot about patience and diplomacy with this project. "Can we consider" gradually replaced "This is the way things are done." Saying the same thing over and over and expecting a different result—the definition of insanity, I knew—gave way to my mother's mantra: "You catch more flies with honey than with vinegar." Even with a more docile composure, I was more than once inadvertently copied on licensee emails complaining about me. Their name calling was unambiguous, nothing was lost in translation. There was a lot of "We know more than that little girl." Repeating myself—and wearing heels—wasn't going to solve this authority issue. So, I went on the offensive.

My research never ended. I spent weekends roaming Barneys, Bergdorf and Sephora, walking out with striped arms covered in shade swatches of Chanel, MAC, NARS, By Terry, Urban Decay and Bobbi Brown. Tom Ford had recently unveiled his "Black Orchid" fragrance in collaboration with Estée Lauder, sparking anticipation for an equally glamorous expansion into makeup. I hoped it would be long after our launch; Ford decamped Gucci after a decade of success and had the Midas touch. While no beauty counter was left unturned as I explored competitors, scrutinized displays and watched women interact with products to further shape my understanding of the market, my own makeup bag remained unchanged.

Bronzer and shiny lips (thanks to the explosion of Lancôme's

Juicy Tubes years earlier) were the look du jour, but I was solely committed to Benefit's Benetint rose-tinted cheek and lip stain and Diorshow mascara. I appreciated makeup as a form of self-expression, much like fashion, but preferred a light touch. Too much not only masked natural beauty but signaled a desire to disguise perceived flaws or deeper insecurities. Years in the industry and multiple rhinoplasties taught me that true beauty is about self-acceptance. I'd come a long way in embracing my looks rather than chasing the unattainable ideal of airbrushed perfection, but I still had insecurities. Fortitude at work, though, helped me care less.

Opting for a natural, rosy glow, I shunned malodorous self-tanners and tanning beds, the cultural phenomenon that made locations so ubiquitous that they became city landmarks. But the quest for a sun-kissed complexion was nothing compared to the reign of thin eyebrows. Ours were waxed (and plucked) to near invisibility in that decade. (Drew Barrymore, Gwen Stefani and even Beyonce sported anorexic arches.) The pencil thin half-moons we sported were only slightly more noticeable than the shaved ones model Kristen McMenamy shockingly showcased on the catwalk at Anna Sui's Fall 1992 collection. (My eyebrows only fully recovered in 2019, thanks to micropigmentation.)

Before famed *New York Times* street photographer Bill Cunningham famously declared, "Fashion is the armor to survive everyday life," I had already learned the transformative power of clothing. For me, fabric provided a sense of strength, shoes instilled confidence and precisely constructed jackets often enhanced determination. I was a soldier and I needed a uniform. As I pushed through, my sartorial shield came from familiar favorites—pressed white shirts and soft cashmere—paired with architectural Calvin Klein pieces that conveyed strength and brand solidarity. I felt a slight reprieve that spring as the makeup line went into production and the ad campaign was shot. It featured newcomer Dutch model Lara Stone, whom *The New York Times* then fashion critic Cathy Horyn called the "anti-model" given her awkward gait, stunned expression and gapped front teeth. She was perfect in the campaign as the imagery was stark, with close-ups showcasing strong makeup looks, reminding consumers this *was* fashion. And a far cry from the nude palettes of the previous attempt.

I leaned into comfort and greater ease of life sporting layered tank dresses and tech-y fabrics that were within my clothing allowance reach—and moved with me. These ensembles mimicked looks I loved previously from Helmet Lang and blended well with easy, breezy tee shirt dresses I picked up from downtown darlings Marc Jacobs and Zero Maria Cornejo. I wanted my outfits to look effortless, though I had never worked so hard in my life.

By fall, mental exhaustion left little room to overthink fashion. I got dressed in the dark for work, slinking to the office in a head-to-toe black uniform which felt less chic and more funereal. Each day I felt less like myself; I had become a walking paper doll. While I had taken a hiatus from writing classes, I continued to journal. It was cathartic and coincidentally provided the makings of a fiction novel. The synopsis? A female fashion executive gets kidnapped and held hostage in a warehouse, forced into cheap labor and poor living conditions. I didn't need a therapist to decipher the meaning behind that plot. My life desperately needed a makeover.

The launch party for our cosmetic collection in Milan at Palazzo Mezzanotte (a.k.a. La Borsa, the Italian stock exchange) should have been the time to celebrate, but something deeper nagged at me as I sipped a sparkling water. The line was certainly bold and impactful—and well received by the press. Doe-eyed Christina Ricci hosted the party that evening. The projected ad campaign shot by David Sims, whom Calvin had discovered and raved about in the early '90s, splashed Lara Stone across the room. Even though I wore a spare, body-hugging black dress and gorgeous funnel neck coat that had just debuted on the runway, my look didn't bring me joy. In fact, it reminded me of what came with the clothing allowance. My life defined by deadlines, achievements, and the thrill of creative pursuits at Calvin was insufficient. And, if I was being honest with myself, unfulfilling. No amount of fashion could conceal a longing for something deeper and more meaningful, beyond the glittering façade of success. And despite my unflagging efforts, there was no guarantee the makeup line was going to triumph.

Milan meets ck Calvin Klein Beauty.

I MUST HAVE LOOKED DEFLATED, despite standing tall in five-inch gray crocodile heels. My boss felt my despair. "You should be proud," she said with a maternal smile as she draped an arm around my shoulders. "Let's enjoy the evening, OK?" I nodded, holding back tears. I knew the first thing I would do once I returned home. After smothering James with hugs, of course, I would retool my resume.

BUT JAMES HAD OTHER PLANS. Before my bags from Milan were even unpacked, I learned he was being relocated to Boston. The financial markets were in flux, thanks to the burgeoning subprime mortgage crisis. Reflecting on my response from one year ago, when my investment banker beau was approached regarding this potential relocation, I could only envision an inferior city dominated by brands specializing in rugby shirts. "Boston? There's no fashion there!" I had said. "My career will be over." But my previous concerns of a sartorial desert did not enter my mind as I was on the verge of my own fashion career crisis. "What will I do there?" I asked quietly. Ever the seer, and a man who wanted only the best for me, James said gently, "Now you can be a writer."

As a Gen-Xer who'd witnessed the divorce rate double and encountered it first-hand when my own parents parted ways before my tenth birthday, a need for independence was etched into the fabric of my identity. Love and dating were fabulous pastimes, but I relegated marriage to the back burner so I could focus on building something larger: a career that ensured autonomy and a sense of accomplishment. At the time, my heroes were women who climbed ladders, shattered glass ceilings and led boardrooms with purpose and poise, not P.T.A. presidents or moms in the sandbox sidelines. Ever since my days of being captivated by Carolina Herrera's runway shows on "Style with Elsa Klensch" my fangirl base had grown to include other female fashion founders, from Miuccia Prada, Donna Karan and Stella McCartney to Cynthia Rowley, Daryl K and Diane von Furstenberg. Add to that list my boss at Calvin.

But what I hadn't yet considered was that their achievements in fashion were equally complemented by strong family values. These women made time to marry and have kids along the way. It made me reconsider my own future, the possibilities that I'd been too hesitant, and maybe afraid, to even consider. Until now—as James stood before me saying, "What do you think?" I had worked so hard to attain success. First patiently waiting and then pouring everything into this dream, shaping it from ambition into reality. This wasn't just a career. Like fashion itself, it was part of my identity. But when it came to love, hadn't I been even more patient? It had been hard to believe I would find a person who saw me—not just their version of what they wanted but flawed, epileptic me—and loved me unconditionally. So maybe I wasn't actually giving anything up. Maybe this career departure wasn't even a risk. Maybe, just maybe, this was the moment everything I deserved would finally come together.

Love won. I packed my bags for Boston and walked away from the high gloss, habitually repainted halls of Calvin Klein. Settling in, finding balance and establishing myself as a writer would take time, courage and motivation, I knew. Sure, I was intimidated. But if I had gleaned anything from the minimalist brand known for reinvention, it was to stay true to myself but always evolve. As Calvin Klein himself told *Women's Wear Daily* in 2000, "Fashion is about change. You have to keep evolving and changing. It has to be new. You have to keep pushing it." While I held onto wearing crisp white shirts and head-to-toe black ensembles, my style—like my goals—would never be static. I knew it would always reflect my current identity, but also serve as a statement for who I was becoming.

I may not have known what was coming next, but I knew this: I'd never succumb to a rugby shirt.

THIRTEEN

Lifelong Love and
Monique Lhuillier Lace

AS THE $64 billion wedding industry continues to thrive, it's still the centerpiece—the wedding dress, of course—that has escalated the price of saying, "I do." OG wedding gown designer Vera Wang paved the way for luxury designers, but it was the shift from '90s minimalism to more opulent, detail-heavy designs with richer fabrics, fuller silhouettes, and overseas production that sent prices soaring. Now, Oscar de la Renta, Carolina Herrera and Monique Lhuillier (whose name is synonymous with lace) have so many betrothed saying "yes" to the $10,000 dress. James proposed in his pajamas, the night before we moved. Despite loving my new fiancée status, it wasn't just lace I loathed but how much meaning a single garment was expected to carry. With a proposal that simple and sincere, I longed for the marriage—not the spotlight or the spectacle of the wedding.

In the two and a half years of dating, James and I had endured my seizure diagnosis, career upheaval, and Ironman training— obviously his avocation, not mine. We cohabitated long enough to build multiple California Closets to accommodate my ever-expanding wardrobe. We were truly building a life together. So when he proposed, the idea of pausing—even momentarily—to focus on wedding planning felt almost unsettling. I had spent years proving that I could flourish without the anchor of tradition. Yet here I was balancing the exhilaration of engagement with the strange dissonance of stepping into an emotional space I had never prioritized. The number of bridal magazines increased from forty in 2000 to a whopping 130 when I got engaged in 2008. Not once did I subscribe or pick up an issue of *Brides* or any other publication devoted solely to one day. I didn't compile tear sheets or mood boards of bridal themes, gowns or rings—and I never yearned for a design inspiration website. (Pinterest didn't even make its debut for another two years.) There was more pressure to make money and strides in my fashion career than to sashay down the aisle. I may have been nearing forty, but by New York City standards, I was virtually a child bride. "What's the rush?" said a (male) friend at Goldman Sachs; "Is this a shotgun wedding?" asked another guy.

I was old enough to know what mattered was not the hundreds of decisions over flowers, lighting, invitation fonts, signature cocktails or seating charts, but rather the promise we were making to each other. Still, I found wedding planning immediately overwhelming. But I made my first vow to James the moment we were engaged. "Let's have a meaningful and small wedding," I whispered to him. And we did. We chose to marry among seventy-five of our loved ones in East Hampton, where we met and once spent summers with friends. I wanted the promise of things to come, life taking off. This did not need to scream "wheels up" as I worried a Hamptons wedding implied, so we planned for it to take place in the fall, the most stunning and quieter season out East. With six months to plan, the tighter timeline would prevent overthinking decisions and incurring additional expenses.

My first creative decision remains my favorite. No, it was not the dress. It was the save-the-date. A 3″ x 3″ white card engraved with three words ("She Said Yes") in clean, modern Helvetica was fastened to a *In the Spirit of the Hamptons* coffee table book with a white paperclip. Calvin himself would have been proud of the minimalist masterpiece. Friends loved the concept, but continually inquired, "What about the dress?" and "Aren't you so excited to find the gown?" How could I say, "Um, no?" How could I explain that as much as I loved fashion, selecting a wedding dress had me flustered? If only I could borrow a dress from the Calvin PR closet as I had done for so many formal events in the past. My stumbling block was far more than an aversion to lace. I had never envisioned myself as a bride—even though I knew I wanted to be married someday. And along with the exorbitant price tag of a gown, it was a lot of undue pressure on one item. Especially for me, a minimalist prone to wearing a version of the same black uniform daily. I'd often wonder, could I pull off a black wedding dress like Sarah Jessica Parker did when she married Matthew Broderick in 1997? (She later admitted that she regretted that decision: "Oh, I wish it was because I was badass. I just was too embarrassed to spend any time looking for a wedding dress.") I could relate.

I always felt that Carolyn Bessette Kennedy, who, much like me, left her fashion job at Calvin Klein to get married, did it right by wearing the simplest of gowns. While struggling with insomnia, frequently envisioning suffocation by tulle and organza, my thoughts repeatedly returned to CBK's sophisticated Narciso Rodriguez sleek silk slip dress. But standing eight inches shorter than the statuesque stunner and sporting a darker blonde than her iconic "child of the beach" sun-dappled hue (as coined by her hair colorist Brad Johns), I knew I'd never edge close to her effortless chic. Even with a slip dress brilliantly cut on the bias.

I had to overcome the idea that a wedding dress was too steeped in emotion. To me, it seemed like a regressive rite of passage and folds of fabric just did not feel like me. I confessed my frustration to my chic friend, Audrey, who had gotten married two years prior. "I know it's just a dress, but it feels so tied up in everything. It's how people will see me, what it says about who I am," I groused.

"Maybe you're overthinking it, she said gently—before raising the bar even higher. "It's not just a dress; it's a statement," she said, as if that explained everything. "It's supposed to encapsulate your essence—or, you know, the glamour version of it."

What did I expect from a woman who worked with Christian Louboutin and whose favorite color was "anything with sparkles." As I was won't to do, I turned to the woman who never steered me wrong—the one who'd once walked down the aisle in a white cake-topper dress, and decades later remarried in a stunning pale gray suit. She knew better than anyone that the dress doesn't make the marriage.

"Hi, Mom."

I WAS among the few who preferred Carrie Bradshaw's original City Hall vintage skirt suit far more than the Vivienne Westwood meringue concoction she wore when Big jilted her. Nevertheless, I wanted to honor tradition. So, I focused on what the ultimate wedding authority, Vera Wang, once said—"Don't disguise yourself"—and made an appointment at a chic, but intimate, fashion-focused atelier. I had zero intention of stepping into the 30,000 square-feet of bridal insanity with thousands of dresses known as Kleinfeld. In my mind, more is never more. Even when it comes to nuptials. James, on the other hand, had his tuxedo—from Calvin Klein Collection Men's, no less—handed to him. I'd won a recent work charity raffle and, along with a gorgeous (though oddly not water-resistant) canoe designed for the Madison Avenue Collection store, I scored a Men's tuxedo designed by the Men's Creative Director, Italo Zucchelli. I accompanied James to the Collection store for his one and only fitting. He had it so easy.

Mark Ingram Atelier, on Madison Avenue near my favorite haunts Bergdorf's and Barneys, opened just after 9/11 when people were very marriage-focused. Ring and gown sales went up, while divorce rates declined by over thirty percent. The brevity of life truly resonated for New Yorkers. Former retail executive and designer Ingram curated the most sophisticated gowns in town.

Renowned for its utterly attentive service, I looked forward to being handled with kid (and white) gloves.

I wasn't a bridezilla; I was fragile.

Some women long to try on dozens of dresses. Me? I wasn't on a journey. I was simply making a decision. One of many. Despite a glut of unsolicited advice from friends about everything from dramatic veils to bridal capes (in case of a fall chill), I adhered to one principle: the dress had to reflect the style I'd spent decades polishing like a precious stone. Forget bubble skirts and bows. My dress had to be breathtakingly simple. A lot to expect from four to eight yards of fabric.

The atelier door opened into a labyrinth of silk and tulle. Dreams, though not mine, of bridal perfection clung to the racks like society women at Le Bernardin. Tradition whispered through the fabric, each gown offering its own quiet promise. But the tension between fantasy and obligation echoed the growing distance I felt between who I was and who I was becoming. For a garment worn fewer hours than a workday, a wedding dress wields a lot of power. I let the heady scent of fresh flowers and the muted hum of classical music wash over me. Audrey was already inside, chatting animatedly with the sales consultant. She waved me over with a grin, her enthusiasm filling the room. "Come on, you have to at least try a few! It's part of the experience," she chirped, pulling me toward a row of gowns that softly beckoned under the boutique's soft lighting.

Immediately, and instinctively, I was drawn to Vera Wang. The gowns were stunning, but the silhouettes—many in strapless designs with velvet sashes—were less than flattering. (I am part of the short torso posse.) I chose three sleeveless sheath dresses, which I had been advised worked better for petite brides, with slight variations. The consultant, armed with a tape measure and an air of omniscient confidence, held up a heap of lace. "This one, sweetie," she pronounced, her voice rich with the authority of someone who'd done this a thousand times. "A gown worthy of an epic woman." I offered a thin smile, quietly amused by the idea that either my dress—or my marriage—required such grandeur. At first glance, there was no cinematic rush of emotion. No bridal cliché or montage set to "Ode to Joy" running through my mind. It was simply stunning. And despite being all lace, it wasn't loud or trying too hard. Like me.

The Monique Lhuillier Scarlet dress was created three years before I slipped into the timeless design, an ivory French lace gown with a Queen Anne neckline and an open back. Today, on the cusp of celebrating my seventeenth wedding anniversary, the designer describes it as one of her most iconic dresses because the unstructured cut is a flattering silhouette on all body types. As I stepped into the dress, I just knew it was the one. Despite its extravagance, it didn't feel attention seeking, nor did it shout for validation. I wasn't transformed. I felt like myself, only prettier. The dress wasn't a costume; it was a mirror.

"It's beautiful," Audrey gushed, her eyes sparkling.

I could have gone barefoot—I was so utterly in love with the dress—but I'd had my eye on the Manolo Feather d'Orsay heels since I'd said, "yes." Along with its inherent opulence, the stunning satin shoe featured a three-and-a-half-inch heel which carried me in comfort not only through the ceremony and late-night dancing, but also into the next iteration of myself. Unlike the dress, I knew I would wear these elegant shoes for decades. I never considered, at that moment, what would happen to my gown in its "I do" afterlife.

WE WED the weekend of the 2008 stock market collapse, which triggered the Great Recession. It was hardly surprising the bridal resale market quickly gained popularity. After having my gown cleaned and preserved by Mark Ingram, I set out to sell. It felt less like surrendering a treasure and more like releasing a symbol that had completed its purpose. While celebs often parted ways with their gowns—Christie Brinkley auctioned hers for The American Red Cross after her husband cheated, while Jerry Hall gave hers to charity as a way to break from her past—I chose to share mine for a different reason. I hoped to offer another bride a piece of its quiet magic, to let someone else to step into its grace and feel, perhaps, that mirror-like reflection of their truest self. Plus, the windfall wouldn't hurt. I was investing in myself by launching my freelance writing career, where—as a newcomer without clips—I was paid in compliments and "exposure," not checks.

Even more love than lace.

As a grail garment, my Monique Lhuillier gown was accepted for resale almost immediately. But at the UPS counter, standing with the oversized box in my arms, I found myself choking up. I could hear the soft swish of the skirt, precisely hemmed to brush just above my Manolos. In my mind, "Ode to Joy" swelled again, as it had when I walked down the aisle.

"Ma'am, excuse me—what insurance do you want for this? How much is this worth?"

What a loaded question. "It's *priceless*," I wanted to say, tempted to bolt.

Instead, I calmly divulged the large sum I'd paid for the gown and then added a modest insurance fee. I patted the box before passing it across the counter and hoped this vestige of my recent past that also nodded to my future would arrive safely. I walked away empty-handed, but not regretful. I knew it had never really been about the dress. I had the marriage of my dreams.

That evening, recounting the moment at the UPS store, my husband turned to me and said quietly, "Please don't sell the dress. It's too important." I was floored. He hadn't weighed in on the resale decision before, but now, his voice was soft, almost protective and tinged with something that surprised me: reverence. I blinked, momentarily unsure of what to say. I'd always thought of the dress as mine: my choice, my expression. But hearing him speak, I realized it had etched itself into his memory too. A freeze-frame of our union. To me, it had been a beautiful dress. To him, it was *the* dress. I contacted the resale founder and asked her to return it to me. She laughed, a little surprised, and said, "You know, no one's ever asked for their dress back."

Today, my wedding gown sits in its archival box. But it's just a keepsake. Seeing it doesn't make me cling to who I once was or how I looked in it. The dress's beauty lies in what it represents. The vows. Our joy. The certainty that we belong together. And while I haven't worn lace since, it still marks how a single garment —worn once, for a single day—can hold within it the beginning of everything.

The Tens

FOURTEEN

Multiples in J.Crew

FASHION DESIGNERS ARE notorious for wearing the same thing every day. Even the world's most visionary beings, with the means and creativity to buy and don whatever they want, build wardrobes around a rotation of crisp white men's shirts, vintage denim and black blazers. Normcore. But with higher thread count. These designers often equate their singular aesthetic to empowerment and confidence—even a home base. I lacked this sartorial stability after I left my career in fashion to become a wife, mother of identical twins, and a Southerner. And all in less than eighteen months. The about face wasn't just a challenge to my psyche. It felt like a threat to my well-established wardrobe.

When Donna Karan unveiled her Seven Easy Pieces collection in 1985, she didn't set out to prescribe a uniform. Instead, she proposed a modern wardrobe philosophy. With just a bodysuit, skirt, tailored jacket, dress, something leather, white shirt and a cashmere sweater, women had a modular system to move effortlessly from day to night, office to evening. Long before terms like "uniform dressing" and "capsule wardrobes" entered the zeitgeist, and subsequently became overused fashion tropes, Karan recognized, and designed to meet, the needs of women leading full, busy lives. "So many women find assembling the right clothes bewildering today," Karan told a reporter at the time. "They've discovered fast ways to put food on the table, but they do not know how to get their wardrobes together easily."

Her collection was seen as revolutionary, yet the irony is that Garanimals had been similarly helping kids mix and match their outfits with ease since the mid-'70s. What made Karan's approach truly unique was her timing. As her collection debuted, the momentum of second-wave feminism was fading, leaving women still grappling with impossible expectations. We were told we could "have it all," but rarely shown how to hold it all together. (Though we are indebted to legendary American designer Claire McCardell, who pioneered American sportswear in the 1940s and famously added pockets so we could actually carry things. Her cotton "Kitchen Dinner Dress" came with an attached apron.) Karan's line may not have resolved the issues surrounding equality, but feeling put together was a start for women. I was barely old enough to vote in 1985, but already I grasped the value of a uniform. To me, it seemed like it wasn't just about getting dressed but about showing up strong.

When Donna Karan built on the success of her Seven Easy Pieces and launched her cooler younger brand DKNY in 1989, I was in college and fully immersed in my own style of uniform: all-American preppy. J.Crew, Duck Head, and Izod Lacoste were daily staples that helped me navigate campus life without compromising who I was trying to become. I wanted to stand out and get good grades in journalism school but not miss too many fraternity mixers. I fantasized about a *Thirtysomething* existence, the yuppie city life complete with that perfect mix of Donna Karan sophistication and Ralph Lauren ease. But for the moment, I was happy to be surrounded by friends and a boyfriend who dressed like clones.

Catalogs, which had existed for over a century, experienced a resurgence in the '80s, thanks to the influx of career women, Maggie Bullock notes in her bestseller *The Kingdom of Prep: The Inside Story of the Rise and (Near) Fall of J.Crew*. Back then,

J.Crew was churning out fourteen catalogs a year, and our dorms and sorority houses were practically wallpapered with its aspirational imagery that was preppy enough to feel polished but without trying too hard. "The catalogs portrayed the delicate brine of a clambake wafting in the air; the particular romance of a misty morning at a rustic lake house," writes Bullock. So true. We gravitated toward sun-bleached chinos, wind-tousled hair and smiles that hinted at summers spent on tony beaches and crisp falls on picturesque campuses. Each spread feeling like an invitation to an effortlessly coordinated life. With so much uniformity, laundry mix-ups were inevitable. Is this my rugby shirt or yours? (Unfortunately, I had yet to discover the magic of a P-Touch label maker.)

Once my uniform had long outgrown collegiate fantasies—thanks to a fashion job, sample sales, and a single-girl savings plan that mimicked Carrie Bradshaw's—every piece in my closet served a purpose. My wardrobe was curated, colorless and befitting my career built around image. As I kidded earlier, getting dressed for work at Calvin Klein was the hardest part of the job. My clothes weren't just an extension of me; they were a strategy. But when James and I relocated to Boston, everything shifted. Without the structure of office life, the rhythm of the city, or the fashion world orbit I'd moved in for years, my once-reliable uniform was unnecessary. We brought, and reinstalled, the California Closets, but they did not get arranged the same; Calvin Klein Collection now lived in the back. I often lingered in front of the beautiful clothes, remembering the ease and confidence they once gave me—now neatly hung but quietly irrelevant, like me.

And yet, there were moments I sighed with relief too, recalling anxieties from clients and late nights. I threw myself into fitness to cope with the emotional free fall of leaving my career—and part of my heart—behind in New York. It gave me structure when everything else felt unmoored, and it became a way to reconnect with my body and rebuild my sense of self. And honestly, part of the appeal was that I didn't have to think about what to wear. As I branched out to train for the Boston Marathon, my wardrobe included more Lycra than ever. The shift felt intentional, and I was in control.

Until I wasn't.

I had grown accustomed to long Saturday runs in ten-degree weather with fellow Team in Training members, coddled by REI apparel hand-selected by my Ironman husband. But the constant nausea was unbearable. Once, on mile sixteen, I ducked into a Starbucks to vomit. This was no hangover. Unless you counted the excessive Swedish fish consumed mid-run; energy gels had not been agreeing with me throughout training.

"You must be pregnant," my mother said, as I lay in bed that afternoon, whining over the phone about my latest hardship, which also included chaffed nipples.

"These are all running-related, Mom," I said, aggravated—all the while making a mental note to get a pregnancy test.

We had just finished writing thank you notes for our wedding gifts and my exquisite Monique Lhuillier gown wasn't even back from the cleaners. There was *no way* I could be pregnant.

But I was.

And in that moment, my identity—already shaky from uprooting my life—came apart at the seams. Suddenly I wasn't just a newlywed adjusting to life in a new city or a former fashion executive trying to make peace with fleece. I was a mother-to-be, stunned into a new reality. I unraveled emotionally as my days became filled with prenatal appointments and perusing baby books. I distracted myself from the growing bulge—which had already popped at six weeks— by obsessing over how to create a nursery in our small Boston apartment. Was there modern furniture that reflected our style yet offered functionality? I was grateful when we ultimately found a Norwegian brand, Stokke, that exceeded expectations. But when even thoughts of sleek Scandinavian oval cribs could not quell my nausea, I stopped in unannounced to the OB's office. There had to be a pill I could take.

"Let's take a look," she said, sing-songing her way over to the sonogram machine. I was already showing at just six weeks. She wanted to ensure everything was okay.

"Well, there's the baby," she said with glee. Her tone shifted when she added, "Annnd there's baby number two."

The oxygen in the exam room seemed to evaporate. I realized I was holding my breath, waiting for her to laugh or admit she'd made an error—a smudge on the screen, maybe? Then, looking deeply into my eyes as if to tell me she'd found cancer, she said, "And there's a third baby." The expletives I uttered in bewilderment were soft, but the first curses my children would ever hear. (And for the record, not the last.)

How was I going to tell James I was carrying triplets? How apropos of me, a perfectionist, to hit the million-and-a-half-to-one odds of having spontaneous triplets. It reminded me of the great Jim Gaffigan joke about kids: "Imagine you're drowning and someone hands you a baby." I was being handed three. She tried to soothe me as I wrangled my clothes back on, promising a proper appointment and conversation once I had digested the sheer lunacy of the news. I murmured, "Sure," and wandered down the hallway in a haze. I made the only phone call that made sense.

"Hi Mom."

From that moment on, everything accelerated. While my intention was to ease into a freelance writing career, pregnancy itself quickly became a full-time job. Monitoring, measuring, managing the disbelief. What I'd envisioned as my creative chapter turned into a clinical one, dictated by ultrasounds, high-risk appointments (thanks to my seizure diagnosis and "geriatric" age of forty), and the quiet thrum of anxiety that comes with carrying three lives at once. And then, when three became two, everything changed again. I went into mourning. I wrapped myself in black Calvin Collection pieces that hadn't been touched since the move. Garments I'd once loved for style, now felt like armor against grief. My running gear was tucked away. I wouldn't be crossing the finish line.

While my belly grew, I refused to buy maternity clothes. Maybe it was denial—I couldn't shake a quiet fear of losing the remaining two babies—or maybe it was pride, as so much had changed already, and the thought of surrendering to elastic panels and empire waists felt like letting go of the last thread tethering me to who I used to be. I made the rounds at Barneys in Copley Place as I sized up in my favorite brands. Oversized Stella McCartney dresses from The Outnet, Net-a-Porter's shopping site featuring past seasons' designer deals, often covered my bump, and I stretched the limits of every waistband I owned. My Seven jeans were slung so low, they revealed a bikini wax update. I knew I was being impractical at times, and I wasn't always comfortable (who is with cankles and adult-onset acne?), but clinging to my clothes from the past gave me the illusion of control.

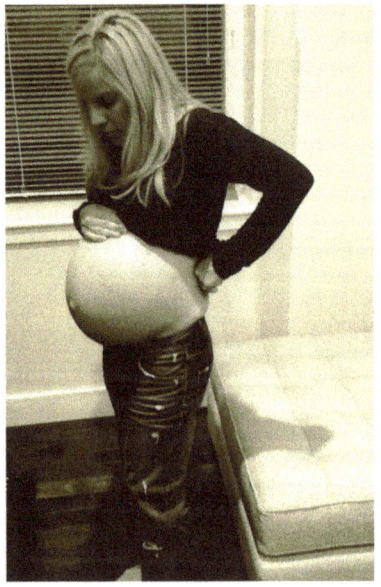

Seven months in (non-stretch) Sevens.

AS MY DELIVERY DATE NEARED, fashion—once my language and livelihood—had become background noise. I clearly wasn't dressing for style. I was dressing to hang on. And yet, in all that discomfort and resistance, something unexpected surfaced: a quieter kind of strength. Not the kind that commands a room in heels or powers through a marathon in sleek leggings, but the kind that endures, even when swollen and uncertain.

And this newfound bravado bubbled up just in time. I had sparingly done some freelance writing and brand development work for Calvin and Juicy Couture, among others, when I was invited to help build a brand for a renowned makeup artist with aspirations of becoming the next Kevyn Aucoin (RIP). It was a dream assignment but came with one caveat: an in-person meeting in New York. I hesitated. Not because I couldn't figure out what to wear—there were enough designer hot-air-ballon-sized dresses available for me. I just wasn't sure I could physically get there. And as I weighed whether or not I could handle the trip, the decision was made for me. At twenty-eight weeks, I was put on bed rest because my cervix was shortening, which could trigger early labor. My next role was clear and all consuming: Full-time mother.

Anyone who has had babies will tell you, "The days are long, but the years are short." I'll add, as I have heard other mothers say: "It nearly broke me—and made me whole." I couldn't tell you when I slept, what I wore or what I ate in that first year. It was all a blur until we moved to Atlanta for James' job, on the cusp of the boys' first birthday. As we marked that milestone, something in me reawakened. I wanted to get dressed again. Power dressing once meant shoulder pads and stilettos. But as a stay-at-home mom of twins in the South still striving to break into fashion writing, it meant something else entirely. My post-pregnancy body had shifted, comfort was non-negotiable, and yet I craved a connection to my old self. I thought back to the one brand that had always brought me joy. I began reaching for J.Crew.

Since its first catalog landed in my mailbox in 1984, J.Crew had quietly shaped my style—and post-birth was no different. With Jenna Lyons now at the helm, the brand reignited my enthusiasm for fashion in a way that honored my new reality, where life was shaped more by routines than runways. Having evolved to fashion-forward preppy and pairing classics in unconventional ways, the brand struck the elusive balance between stylish and practical; living proof that chic could coexist with spit-up and sleepless nights. I stocked up on pieces that could handle a stroller walk or a rare coffee date. Army surplus jackets, a nod to a Baltimore haunt from my youth (Sunny's Surplus), and schoolboy blazers paired with striped tees and broken-in denim became my cool-weather uniform. I settled in, and easily nursed babies, in chambray shirts and tissue tees paired with four-inch chino shorts in every hue as temps rose. Cashmere sweaters in an array of neutrals and striped button-down shirts found their way into my closet, often paired with slouchy khakis; a little wrinkled but always anchored in good taste, and so easy to wash after crawling through park slides to collect toddlers in dirty diapers. My uniform was as much about comfort as clarity, showing up fully for my family while trying to honor the ambitious woman I still was underneath. Motherhood hadn't diminished my minimalist instincts though, and even with babies in tow, I happily opted out of the era's bubble-necklace craze.

I wasn't zipping through Bendel's researching beauty anymore or primping for a night out, but I still found a way to shine with J.Crew's signature lipstick—a bright, poppy orangey-red called "George" and created by the brand's makeup mastermind, Troi Ollivierre. I hadn't pursued the makeup artist project during my pregnancy, but celebrating the launch of this line brought back the thrill—and the heartache—of what it takes to bring a beauty brand to life. My Calvin experience had shaped me, but it had also left its mark. It stung to hear the ck Calvin Klein line was shuttered two years after I left, though strangely, the news also affirmed I'd chosen the right path in walking away.

As my babies grew from fragile, NICU newborns into curious

little boys with endless questions and scraped knees, I slowly began to reclaim more than just my wardrobe. I was reclaiming my sense of self. Motherhood had swept me into a tidal wave of responsibilities that demanded everything: my time, my energy, and my identity. Fashion (and some days, even getting dressed) represented a distant luxury. My carefully curated closet felt like a remnant from a version of me I could barely remember. I'd think how silly and self-absorbed, I'd once been in thinking that deciding what to wear to Calvin felt like the hardest part of my day. I hadn't known that the true luxury was not the clothes themselves, but the time to linger over what to wear.

While finding my footing, I leaned on the incredible famil-iarity of crisp white shirts, made wearable thanks to Jenna's iconic sleeve roll, even while sporting carpal tunnel syndrome surgery casts on both wrists. (Double burping is not for the weak.) In those days of endless multitasking with a boy on each hip, I was most grateful for a J. Crew uniform that offered one less thing to solve, and just enough polish to feel like myself. It took time but I learned that motherhood didn't mean leaving behind who I was despite my significant sartorial shift. My world had narrowed but style wasn't in the rearview; it was mine to define again. Rebuilding a wardrobe helped bridge the woman I had been with the one I was still becoming—not erasing the former, just redrawing the lines.

But it wasn't just my wardrobe that needed redefining. I faced my fears and began writing—not as a side hustle, but as some-thing with deeper meaning. I ignored the sage advice to "sleep when the babies sleep" to pitch essays to *The Boston Globe*, *The New York Times*, and reached out to former Calvin colleagues to network. No longer tethered to clients, I had the freedom to align with brands and craft stories that reflected my values and served real women. With more than a decade of exposure to beauty and (anti-)aging, I wanted to capture the sharp shift I was experi-encing in my forties. I felt driven to reshape how growing older is portrayed as defeat in the media. I took on fun fashion assignments from French Connection UK and Juicy Couture, contributed each summer to a Hamptons publication, and eventually found a home at *The Fine Line*—a (now defunct) publication that embraced women over forty as the healthy, wealthy and stylish women we are—sans the anti-aging messages.

My freelance writing work grew alongside my boys' expanding worlds, and so did my style—evolving from pure functionality into something more elevated, more intentional. I stopped dressing just to get through the day and started dressing to feel creative and productive, especially as I wrote from the comforts of home. Jenna Lyons didn't just inspire outfits—she inspired *permission:* To dress for joy. To clash on purpose. To wear a gold lamé pencil skirt even if your only appointment that day was the post office. While I personally veered away from lamé, I did indulge in statement pants—a growth engine for J.Crew (a category that drove sales and became a signature of the brand) that made me nostalgic for my younger days wearing Cynthia Rowley's map pants. J.Crew showed at Fashion Weeks selling head-to-toe looks, and I was all in. From cropped slim-fitting pants that grazed the ankle to voluminous trousers, all mixed and matched with the brand's love affair with color—pink, punchy yellow and other jewel tones. I wore turtlenecks, sweater vests, more boyfriend blazers. Collars popped, of course.

What I loved most about this wardrobe was that it became my latest uniform — but not one of uniformity. It was embellished prep and tomboy faves that married my former New York edge to my relocated southern persona. I felt intimately drawn to fashion again—not to prove something to others, but as a reflection of who I had become: a wife, a mother, and now a writer establishing her voice and dreaming of writing a fashion essay collection. Jenna Lyons said it best in her *Man Repeller* interview during this time: "Finding your own way to feel beautiful is important." I did just that. And I had the honor of telling her firsthand the impact she had on me when I told her about this very book.

I am still a proud J.Crew devotee today. When the glorious

catalog made a comeback in Fall 2024, with sixty-one-year-old Demi Moore gracing the cover, I felt more than nostalgia, I felt pride. With Olympia Gayot as creative director, the brand continues to carry the torch for womenswear that reflects how we actually live. As she's a fellow twin boy mom, I felt seen. Gayot designs with the realities of motherhood in mind, but it's her ethos that resonates most. "There's so much creativity coming from women, especially mothers," she once said.

Fashion has always told us to dress for the job we wanted. But what if we dressed for the life we're living—and are still shaping? Some days, that means reaching for something from my life in New York: the Dior trench I snagged while working Seventh on Sale, the urban-myth Manolo Mary Janes, the anthracite wool funnel neck coat purchased with my Calvin clothing allowance. Other days, a threadbare Gap navy cotton sweater carries me just as far. Because while I learned to run in heels at Calvin Klein, I learned to stand still in that sweater. To be present, grounded and fully myself in a life shaped more by nap schedules and school drop-offs, than fashion-driven deadlines and launch dates.

Embracing a uniform has never been about limiting creativity or expression; it's about showing up fully as the women we are. And the ones we're still becoming. I am on the precipice of big things; I can feel it. And with my uniform on, I'm dressed for what's next.

The Present

FIFTEEN

Open Minded

DR. DANIEL GILBERT, a Harvard psychologist and self-described "happiness expert," delivered a 2014 TED Talk titled "The Psychology of Your Future Self" that went viral—and opened my eyes to my own personal evolution. In it, he explains we make decisions throughout life to shape the person we hope to become, yet we also assume that we have just become the person we were meant to be—and will never change. He calls this false assumption the "end of history" illusion and he debunks it by showing how much we actually change—day to day, decade to decade. Everything from our values to our favorite vacation spots shifts as we age. I am living proof. Since strutting down the jetway with my Ann Demeulemeester hanging bag, I've evolved profoundly, both personally and professionally. Time has brought not only rewarding work in fashion but also a reckoning.

I took a leap of faith after leaving Calvin to pivot back to my first love (and college degree), journalism. What started in the margins, pitching stories on the side, has become what defines me. Writing gives me both the creative outlet I crave and allows me to champion an aging generation determined not to fade quietly, but to be seen, heard, and celebrated. Along the way, I also took emotional risks, opened my heart to love, and discovered who I was and what I was worth. Finally. But as Dr. Gilbert (and David Bowie), remind us, "Time may change me" Research shows that we remember who we were, but struggle to imagine who we'll become. I have a strong feeling I'll be happy. And wearing a crisp white shirt, of course.

Change has a sense of humor. A surprising new garment entered my wardrobe once I'd fully settled in Atlanta and sent my twin boys to school: an apron. A full-coverage, ties-at-the-waist apron from Williams-Sonoma—hardly where I imagined buying apparel—now stained with pancake batter. (Of course, I now have my eye on a James Perse striped, half apron in Belgian linen, a clear departure from the days I frequented the East Hampton store in search of utility pants and tees that nailed effortless California minimalism.) When I first tied on the apron, it was like dressing in a costume. As if I were playing the part of a domestic goddess I hadn't auditioned for (although who doesn't aspire to be, in some ways, more like Ina Garten or Martha Stewart, two of the most prominent and successful lifestyle moguls). But some-where, amidst juggling pots and pans, while wearing elbow-length yellow gloves to clean dishes, I began to feel awash with calm. My ambition and attitude shifted. I had nothing to prove—and every-thing to gain.

While I once stored Calvin Klein Collection shoe boxes in an oven, that appliance now produces creations from *Half-Baked Harvest*. I bake from scratch, source seasonal produce, and yes, frequently use a slow cooker. My devotion to style remains. It just followed me into the kitchen. Under the apron, my look has shifted too. Comfort gained an edge. I started living in Isabel Marant because no one channels a cool Parisian tomboy quite like she does with her nonchalant but decidedly chic designs. Comfort didn't replace confidence. It just reimagined it. Ann Mashburn became a staple—and supplier of my Marant. Mashburn, a former fashion editor-turned-retailer curates elevated basics that move seamlessly from school drop-off to dinner out. Not to mention, her endless versions of the "drink and pray dress," a modest but modern shift perfect for going straight from cocktails to confession—or vice-versa. My beloved mainstay, J.Crew, now pairs easily with an ever-growing Adidas collection. With or without the Gucci collab, the sneakers work. The retro Sambas alone can be their own mood board: swap the laces, change the vibe.

I now frequent consignment stores the way I once stalked sample sales. Out went the Veronica Beard blazers that no longer buttoned without protest, along with the Theory trousers that felt, frankly, unforgiving. In came a COS corduroy blazer straight out of *The Official Preppy Handbook*, Gucci platforms that lift spirits and height, and soft button-downs that double as pajamas on long days. I sometimes wondered if the swaps were betrayals of my old self. Not at all. I now realize I wasn't vanishing or erasing my identity. I simply edited my closet and my life. These days, the SUV might give me away, but don't be mistaken: this is off-duty model meets on-duty mom. Watch your tone—and your turn signal.

For years, I measured my worth by the clothes I wore—and often, the career they outfitted. Learning to separate the two took time and some humility; I've finally untangled the belief that my sartorial choices define me. And how I perceive others. Aging, in its quiet wisdom, continues to reveal that style is only part of the story for every woman. Fashion remains a joy, and forever a powerful outlet for self-expression, but it no longer takes center stage. Now, I see the richness of life in those we hold close, not the labels we wear. It sounds like something my Southern mother-in-law might embroider on a throw pillow—and yet, somehow, it's true. This shift happened quietly, sneaking in like a smattering of gray hair or laugh lines. Where once my clothes had to make a declaration—"I am competent. I am creative. I am someone you should take seriously"—they now feel more like parentheses. A soft aside. Fashion is no longer a front for me.

I'm perfectly capable of showing—and speaking—up for myself. In fact, I've fashioned a successful career out of my naked voice. Even if writing this book, which began with one uncertain essay written in 1998, felt a lot like stripping down in front of a mirror. Whereas I once presented beauty strategies and guided fashion clients, I now speak to a larger purpose (and dare I say, a dream): exploring fashion, beauty, and wellness through the lens of aging. What started as a personal evolution has become my public forum, bringing editorial opportunities and a chance to rewrite the narrative of growing older. Instead of focusing on fashion's fleeting obsessions, I now champion its enduring role and truths: the confidence it brings, the curiosity it sparks, and the courage it gives us to keep evolving.

While Dr. Gilbert finds that change is a constant, our evolution still demands intention—a truth I see reflected in Maria Cornejo, the Chilean American designer behind the Zero + Maria Cornejo label who opted to focus solely on her bestselling styles after nearly thirty years in fashion. Always a fan of her sculptural silhouettes, commitment to sustainability, and unwavering independence, I'm sure Cornejo's pivot wasn't just about simplifying —it was about courage: knowing what works, standing by it, and having the certainty to let the rest go. That clarity defines my own tightly edited closet now. I happily ignore most trends and vehemently shun cultural vernacular like "age appropriate." Instead, I just wear what I love. Repeatedly.

I remain a minimalist—my small rebellion, my choice in how and when I evolve—but I'm anything but beige. So, when the quiet luxury trend showed up dressed up in greige, I put it on mute. Fashion is fickle, and trends will always shift, but true style refuses to stay subdued. It can be bold (yes, even in neutrals), unapologetic, and entirely its own. Once you commit to your own personal look, it never loses its voice. As fashion designer Claire McCardell said in her 1956 book (reissued in 2022), *What Shall I Wear?*: "Fashion is a continued story—and a continuing one. It is birth and reincarnation, more positive than negative, never really arbitrary. That's the exhilaration of it all; that's the challenge and the fun. Keep remembering that Fashion is fickle, that it changes constantly, never stands still. Take advantage of its flexibility and make some new rules."

AND WHILE I'VE long argued—and written repeatedly—that the concept of "age-appropriate" has no place in fashion, it persists. Not on coverlines, given print media's decline, but more insidiously in conversations, marketing campaigns, dressing rooms, and even our own internal monologues. Fashion was never meant to be about rules. At its core, fashion is about self-expression. At every and any age. Your style does not expire with milestone birthdays. I've always felt "dressing your age" is less about style and more about society's discomfort with aging, particularly for women. How dare a woman show her legs, sport long hair, or go sleeveless? I've never felt more at home in my clothes than I do now—not because I've learned to "dress my age," but because I've stopped caring about being typecast by my appearance. It's society's way of edging out women. And I refuse to fade.

Recently, I nearly slid off my Lucite Louis Ghost Chair while watching Hollywood stylist Karla Welch's MasterClass when she said, "You don't need to have style to have a great life." Coming from someone who built her career on style, that sentiment hit hard. But that radical thinking is exactly what makes Welch, who works with clients Tracee Ellis Ross and Sarah Paulson, an icon. Style isn't essential—but it holds real power. Because, coming full circle, Fashion (yes, always with a capital F) is not frivolous. And this book, written over a span of almost three decades, is a testament to the fact that style is as much a journey as life itself. I've found identity, strength, and peace in how I present myself to the world. Personal style tells a story, but it's never the whole story. It's merely the wrapping paper, the fold, the tape. The real gift is who we become while deciding what to wear. My silhouette no longer speaks solely for me, but my clothes still tell my story. When I penned my first essay, I thought I wanted to write a book about fashion. What I ultimately learned through my thoughts and words is that I had to write a book about becoming.

BUT I WON'T EVER FORGET the carefree girl who extended simple airport security into a marathon in Fiorentini + Baker moto boots, while my husband patiently waited, lugging twenty pounds of *Italian Vogue* and *French Elle* magazines. Or the girl who chose whimsy over conformity in her Cynthia Rowley pants, Marc Jacobs jeans and Tory Burch caftans—all while learning to love herself enough to evolve. And that growth brought new aspirations, Just as I once took notes watching Elsa Klensch report on runways and studied fashion like it was a science, I later dove into night classes with a literary agent to help coax this fashion essay collection to life. Through writing and sharing my story here and in my career, I'm reclaiming what I didn't tell B decades ago in that Chicago apartment. He was right. I did want to be a model. But not the leggy gazelle who walks a runway. I wanted to become a *role model*. The one who walks women through what comes after—the years when confidence replaces collagen. The one who empowers women to stop asking for permission and to just show up—lived-in, experienced and entirely on her own terms.

Ironically, just as I thought I'd mastered this self-acceptance, life shifted once again. Menopause, aging, motherhood—each reshaped me (in menopause's case, quite literally), sometimes dramatically. Menopause didn't knock—it bulldozed. It tore through my closet and body like a wrecking ball of hot flashes, insomnia and brain fog. Clothes that once made me feel invincible now clung in the wrong places or sagged in others. I missed my waistline, sure, but I mostly missed feeling in sync with my reflection. I had always loathed belts (again, short torso posse) but this shapeshifting banished them once and for all. My arms wanted nothing to do with cap sleeves. And don't get me started on underwire bras—medieval torture devices disguised as lingerie. Thankfully, High Sport kick flare pants arrived—soft, stretchy and mercifully forgiving. But of course, I bought the J.Crew version.

This book details my escapades in love and ambition, but fashion has endured as one of my longest and most loyal relationships. My looks are a visual diary of every version of myself. And just a glance in my closet reveals how I've matured. I no longer need to seek attention; I am visible to those who matter. I don't demand perfection. I celebrate presence. I don't believe in "the one that got away"—not a boyfriend, a job or a blazer. I am exactly where I am meant to be, wearing what belongs on me. Eleanor Roosevelt once said, "Happiness is not a goal; it's a by-product of a life well lived." The same goes for our style—it naturally emerges when we're honest about who we are and the life we want to lead. As I careen toward sixty, I know I will change again —and continue to lovingly embrace the stylish, successful woman I am becoming. Because while I've spent a lifetime being clothes minded, measuring myself by what I wore, today I embrace being open minded.

Famous Last Words

Christine Morrison

AUTHOR

YOU'VE HEARD MY STORY–THE clothes I loved, the ones I let go, the people and places that shaped me—and the version of myself I uncovered along the way. If I were to leave you with one piece of style advice, it's this: let wanderlust be your stylist. Let curiosity guide your choices. Open your closet the way you'd open a map—with heart, imagination, and a willingness to explore. Sometimes, what you pull off the hanger is more than just an outfit. It's a reminder of where you've been and a quiet invitation to where you're going next.

Sarah Clary

STYLIST

STARTING IN MIDDLE SCHOOL, I ran my closet with the precision of a military operation and the drama of a Broadway production. I even had a calendar—an actual, physical calendar—where I logged every outfit I wore down to the shoes, accessories, even hair clips. This wasn't just a style diary; it was evidence. Because the number one rule was simple: thou shalt not repeat a look too soon.

And if I did repeat? Oh no, I was not walking into school with the exact same outfit twice. No, ma'am. That skirt would get a new co-star, the sweater would suddenly be layered over a turtleneck, and the shoes swapped for something louder, shinier—maybe even impractical enough to guarantee I'd trip going up the stairs.

AT FIRST, the whole thing was pure defense strategy. I was skinny, hated my face and still waiting for puberty to call. Clothing became my distraction—my way of saying, "Don't look at my body or face. Look at my outfit." I could pretend the fabric was doing all the talking, and I was just...hosting the conversation.

But then something shifted. Somewhere between Monday's

"preppy cool" and Friday's "mysterious art student" phase, I realized this wasn't just about covering up. It was about creating. My calendar wasn't a list of outfits—it was a collection of characters I got to play. I started seeing possibilities in everything. A button-down shirt wasn't just a shirt—it could be worn open over a dress, tied at the waist with high-waisted jeans, layered under a sweater with the collar peeking out, or even tucked in backward for a "What is she doing?" moment. Each piece of clothing felt like a story waiting to be told.

AND THAT'S what hooked me—the storytelling. A denim jacket could turn a dress from prim to effortless, a belt could reshape a silhouette—and somehow shift my posture along with it. A new color could make me feel louder or quieter, braver or softer.

Every morning became a kind of creative rehearsal: Who am I today? What's my role? Do I need armor, or do I want to float? I cycled through personas: the rebel in ripped jeans, the minimalist who pretended she read *The New Yorker*, the sporty girl in sneakers who could actually run from point A to point B (though I preferred to walk slowly for the aesthetic).

Without realizing it, I was in training. I was honing an eye for proportion, texture and mood—skills I would later use as a stylist and creative consultant. Back then, I just thought I was trying not to get roasted in the cafeteria. Turns out, I was building a creative practice.

LOOKING BACK, that calendar wasn't about vanity. It was about vision. Each page proved that I could take a single item, imagine endless possibilities and tell a different story every day. Clothes were never just clothes—they were my first language, my first stage, and my first act of authorship. They still play those roles. Now, I use them to evoke feeling or lighten life's weight—sometimes that means throwing on sequins. It may seem silly, but there's power in it, and in small ways, it still helps the middle schooler in me and the adult I am today.

SO MY ADVICE? Treat your life like a conspiracy board: mix the suspects, change the plot twists, make the ending impossible to guess. Wear the ridiculous shoes to carpool. Throw on sequins to buy milk. The truth is, life will always try to put you in a box—so you may as well show up in something so loud, so unapologetic, they'll have to build a bigger box.

Stacy London

TV PERSONALITY, AUTHOR, STYLIST,
MID-LIFE/MENOPAUSE ADVOCATE

I WORKED in the fashion industry right when Grunge hit the scene. The legendary 1990s. In one way, I felt lucky. I could afford oversized flannel plaid shirts from thrift stores and peasant skirts from Bleecker Street and still copy a high-designer look, even if I couldn't afford or fit into high-designer sizing. But on the other hand, I was a size sixteen, which was almost unheard of in the industry at the height of heroin chic. There was no body positivity or acceptance back then. In fashion, exclusivity was the point. Clothes were expensive, and size ranges were limited. I always suspected people made fun of me behind my back—honestly, who knows.

I DON'T KNOW exactly when I started to hate my body, but I think it was around eight or nine years old. I'm not sure why. My psoriasis didn't show up until a few years later, so I don't know what triggered that early dislike of myself. I just remember feeling that I wasn't as pretty as my classmates; I wasn't as thin or athletic as the other girls. I didn't know how to accessorize with the cool barrettes or socks like they did.

THE NEGATIVE SELF-TALK I developed at an early age made
me hypersensitive to other people's opinions—or at least what I
assumed they thought of me. Being surrounded by the beauty and
perfection of the fashion world only reinforced the idea that,
because I didn't look like those who worked within it, I wasn't as
valuable as they were.

It's taken me years to separate the beauty and artistry of style
from how I feel about myself — to understand that my feelings
determine what is and isn't beautiful to me. That's my choice, not
the choice of an industry or anyone else's opinion. That, to me, is
real style: belonging to yourself.

Nikki Kule

FOUNDER, KULE

I'VE ALWAYS LOVED STRIPES. They've followed me through every stage of my life. I can trace almost every era of my style back to a stripe: the navy-and-cream sailor top I wore as a kid that my parents brought me back from Portofino, the French-inspired tees that filled my closet in college, the crisp button-downs I wore to my first job in fashion, and now, the bold pattern that has become a signature of my brand, KULE.

Over the years, I've collected stripes from different designers and places: Marni in the late '90s was one of my favorites. Later, Phoebe Philo's Celine gave me some of my favorite pieces. And then there are the discoveries from my travels, found in small shops tucked away in France and Italy, each one tied to a memory. My closet is full of special pieces that tell my story.

WHAT I LOVE MOST about stripes is how familiar yet fresh they can feel. They're graphic without trying too hard, timeless without being boring. A stripe can live in so many styles and still feel completely relevant. I think that's why they've always been my constant.

When I started KULE as a children's wear company almost

twenty-five years ago, my very first collection included little striped rugbies with matching diaper covers. From that moment on, every collection featured at least one stripe. So, stripes became part of my brand naturally. Every time I designed a collection, I found myself drawn back to them. They made me happy. And once you find something that consistently makes you happy, you lean in.

MY LOVE of stripes extends beyond fashion. I love stripes in interiors—on a sofa, a rug, or a lampshade. They bring structure but also play. They can make a space feel pulled together or a little cheeky, depending on the color and scale. I think of stripes as visual punctuation: a rhythm that keeps things interesting.

Even in art, stripes always catch my eye. For example, some of my favorite artists—Tanya Ling, Sydney Albertini and Frances Featherstone—all use stripes as an integral part of their work. It's where my eye connects and where it resonates for me.

At home, in my closet, or on the walls of a favorite exhibit, stripes make me feel grounded. They remind me that good design doesn't need to be complicated to be impactful—it just has to feel like you.

WHEN PEOPLE THINK of KULE now, they often think of stripes, and I couldn't be happier about that. They represent everything I want the brand to be: optimistic, effortless and unmistakably a part of me.

SO YES, I'll always love stripes. They've been my pattern, my palette and my point of view. They're simple lines, but to me, they're the happiest lines.

Meg Strachan

FOUNDER, DORSEY

I GREW up watching my grandmother get dressed. In wide-leg trousers, in beautiful blouses, always watching the way her bag hung so effortlessly from her shoulder. Even as a child, I noticed the smallest details: how she folded her sweaters, how she placed her jewelry in tiny Italian bowls beside the sink at the end of the day. As I got older, I wanted to do the same. Getting dressed became a ritual, first a way to express myself, then a kind of armor. In the early years of my career, clothing was how I showed the world I could lead.

BUT WHEN I BECAME A MOTHER, especially to a little girl, I realized getting dressed was something deeper. It was a way to return to myself. Watching her try on sparkle, tutus and super-hero costumes reminded me what fashion really is: an act of becoming. Each outfit a small declaration of presence and a way to explore who we are and who we might be.

AS MY PERSPECTIVE CHANGES, I trust that what I wear will evolve as I do.

April Gargiulo

FOUNDER, VINTNER'S DAUGHTER

WE LIVE in a world bombarded with twenty-four-hour newness, and that relentless churn drives twenty-four-hour sameness. In a frantic bid for our attention, products are made faster and cheaper than ever. The result is a flattening of true craftsmanship into false content. Fashion may have reached this point before beauty, but now the industrial cycle of new and next is impacting everyone. Finding the true and the beautiful has become more difficult with each passing year. When I come across something crafted with real loving intent, it feels almost like a relic from another time. I know how rare it is for something to live up to that high level of discernment, so I want to hold onto it, protect it —and at the same time—share it with everyone I know.

BUT FOR YEARS, I was trapped in the same cycle of "new, more, next." When my friends were buying absurdly expensive hand-bags, I was buying absurdly expensive skincare. Each month, I would explore the newest "innovation" promising instant results and almost every time, the results were the same as the month before. This went on for years, until my husband and I were on a trip to Marrakesh.

WHENEVER I TRAVEL, I love to visit old apothecaries—the kind women have been shopping in for decades, even centuries. This is how I found myself in a 200-year-old shop with dozens of different shapes and sizes of glass bottles, each hand-marked in Arabic, which I sadly do not speak. The beautiful shop owner also spoke Arabic, so we communicated with hand signals. I kept pointing to my acne and she kept giving me a bottle of oil. Each time I pointed again, she offered me the same bottle, smiling insistently.

I cannot emphasize enough how terrifying it was to think about putting oil on my face back then. I grew up in an era where I was taught to dry out my oily skin to the point of irritation and flaking. Sea Breeze, Stridex pads and alcohol were the tips and tricks of the time for acne-prone skin. I look back on it now and cringe of course, but this was what we were all taught. Putting the contents of this bottle on my face felt terrifying, but I thanked the shop owner and went to our hotel. That night, like someone jumping out of a plane for the first time, I held my breath, applied the oil and prayed.

I woke up the next morning and was shocked. I had fully expected to see my skin erupt with angry bumps, but instead it was the most balanced and calm I had seen in years. And as I always say, once you use oil, you can never go back.

THIS EXPERIENCE LED to the creation of Vintner's Daughter and underscored the lessons I learned from growing up in a wine-making family. Listening to the wisdom of our ancestors and our earth is critical. Quality cannot be rushed. To make the very finest, you must be uncompromising in your values. For me, this means creating products with deep resonance and respect for our skin, our spirits and our world. Because I don't want to make anyone's next product, I want to make their last and forever products.

THE FEELING that comes from this kind of commitment is one of deep trust. It is ultimately what I and so many women like me want from our beauty choices. We are highly discerning and not fooled by the circle of sameness cloaked in "innovation." We are searching for those rare, beautiful and well-made things that truly deserve to be a part of our life. They are harder to discover, but thankfully, there is joy in the hunt.

FOR ANYONE who's feeling caught in the cycle of urgency, false promises and the fear of missing out: Pause. Trust your intuition. Let it guide you toward what speaks to your senses and your values. The truth is, real beauty—and anything truly worthy—requires patience. And that is the kind of beauty that never goes out of style.

Megan Papay

CO-FOUNDER, FRĒDA SALVADOR

IN 1998, I worked in the celebrity styling department at Calvin Klein. After the Spring/Summer show, I went to the after-party at Milk Studios wearing a white Calvin Klein tank undershirt, dark skinny jeans and neon green snakeskin stilettos. I will never forget that outfit. It made me feel magnetic. I still have the tank...I wish I still had the shoes, because looking back, the outfit was so simple —it was the shoes.

BEFORE FRĒDA, I worked in almost every industry of fashion: PR, freelance styling, personal shopping and I even ran my own handmade accessories line that sold to stores like Henri Bendel. After moving from the East Coast to San Francisco with my husband, I started over again and was hired by a footwear designer as her full-time stylist. Eventually, I became her fashion director.

That's where I met Cristina Palomo Nelson, my FRĒDA co-founder. She's a third-generation shoemaker and we clicked immediately. We traveled together to Italy for sourcing and production, and during those trips, we'd constantly talk about what we would do differently if we had our own brand. She always knew she wanted to start one. I didn't know I was on the same trajectory until I met her. We started FRĒDA SALVADOR in 2011 with a clear mission: to build a brand and a community of women from the ground up.

TODAY, I co-design all of our collections with Cristina and I also lead brand, community and style our campaign shoots. My background in styling goes all the way back to my undergraduate degree in costume design at the University of Virginia, where I studied the "Psychology of Dress" and how clothes help shape identity and tell a story. I've always been interested in how style makes you feel, and that consideration 100 percent drives my work and my personal style.

THERE'S a concept called *enclothed cognition*, which is basically the science behind why the right outfit can change your mood, your confidence, even your posture. I think about that every single day when designing, styling, shopping and especially when getting dressed in the morning. That's why personal style is so important to me. It's not about trends at all—it's about discovering what makes you feel happy, strong, grounded and ready for your day. And that's so personal. It's truly what makes YOU feel good.

I AM the first to admit, I love the power of influence. I get inspired all of the time by my favorite personalities on Instagram or street style. But it's not about wanting what they have because of their credentials. It's about getting inspired to try something new, remembering something in my closet, or my favorite: evoking a memory that puts me in a really fun time or place. I love the power of nostalgia. So many pieces in my closet (most of them, actually) carry a story that 100 percent affects how I show up that day. Or sometimes it's simply a color. I have an angora sweater from Rachel Comey that is the identical shade of blue to the water in the Abacos, Bahamas, which is my happy place. I wear this sweater when I have to do something out of my comfort zone, like for public speaking. It takes me to a place where I feel my best, and that serenity gives me the grounding confidence to shake off the nerves. It's wild, try it! I also now look for this color when shopping. I love how I feel in this vibrant color.

EACH MORNING when I go into my closet, it's almost intuitive. Something will pop out at me. It's a feeling. Then I dress around it. Nine times out of ten, I start with a pair of shoes. So yes, I love shoes—I always have. But what I really love is the feeling they unlock.

I AM HONORED to be part of this collection of essays. Inspiring women to discover the power of personal style is so important to me. Your day starts there. The way you show up begins there. And this is not an aspirational exercise; discovering your personal style is not tied to a large clothing allowance (thankfully!). It's a powerful mindset and I encourage you all to indulge it. Take a minute for yourself each morning. Think about your day and how you want to feel. Then, choose an outfit that embodies that feeling—and why not start with a killer pair of shoes?

Meg Younger

FOUNDER, JEAN GENIE VINTAGE CO.

ALTHOUGH I GREW up in a small town in Oklahoma, Skatetown was a vibrant scene filled with kids of all ages. It wasn't just for the little tykes—high schoolers ruled the rink in those days. It was there that I got my first glimpse of the trends of the time—more precisely, the vibe of what the alternative cool kids were wearing. They all skated in denim. Middle America '80s street style in its truest form.

I WAS ONLY SEVEN, but my eyes were wide open, and I paid attention. I watched with curiosity and awe as the older girls commanded attention shuffle skating in their tight skinny jeans. Guess jeans were the ultimate status symbol, and I knew I had to have zippers at my ankles and that little triangle on my back pocket. The only problem? They cost $45, and my allowance was a sad $5 a month.

My mom soon realized this wasn't a passing phase, as I saved for almost a year until I could afford those life-changing jeans. They were absolutely worth the wait and the painful anticipation. The moment I slipped them on, I immediately felt cool, and for the first time, experienced what a perfect pair of jeans can do for your self-confidence and outlook on life.

MY OBSESSION with denim only grew from there. Never one to don dresses or skirts unless required by a specific holiday or event, I religiously stayed on top of denim trends and designers, saving every dollar for the pairs that spoke to me. At first, it was about the cool factor and fitting-in, but eventually it became my identity. My blossoming style offered me a way to show my individuality through clothing. I didn't want to look like everyone else. Still don't. This is a huge reason why I love vintage: the one-of-one is the easiest way to stand out in a sea of sameness.

DENIM WAS, is and always will be the foundation of whatever outfit or look I create. It's the anchor thanks to its versatility, comfort and timelessness. Nothing feels better than a perfectly worn and faded pair of blue jeans. With so many styles, washes and fits, any BODY can find a pair of jeans that makes them feel empowered. Denim is both a neutral base to build upon AND the key piece that takes center stage. It can exude femininity or allow you to tap into androgyny.

USUALLY, my first decision is to choose the pair of jeans that best fits how I'm feeling that day. This strategy rarely fails me. If you're struggling to pick your jeans, don't worry—everyone's been there. You don't need a different pair for every day! Build a denim capsule collection with timeless styles. Five pairs are all you really need:

- **A fitted straight-leg in a medium blue wash**. (My rec: vintage Levi's 501) These will be your workhorse. The versatility knows no bounds.
- **A black wash straight-leg**. These take you from Kate Moss rocker style to Victoria Beckham classic and polished with a dash of mystery.
- **A bootcut or flare in a medium to dark wash**. Whether you wear flip flops or boots, this cut elongates your legs.
- **A baggy or boyfriend straight-leg in light to medium wash with good fades**. Pair with sneakers, sandals or ballet flats—they can be rolled up or bunched at the ankle. Your "sweatpants" denim option. Throw on a heel and you might be surprised by how sexy the contrast feels.
- **Let your personal style complete your collection**. They can follow the current trend or your mood. It might be a skinny jean if that's what you're feeling, or a pair of raw denim. Distressed your vibe? Go for it!

ALMOST EVERY PAIR of jeans I've ever purchased just because someone else had them, or solely to follow a trend, eventually ended up in the donation or resale pile. Your jeans should be as personal as your hairstyle or your home décor. They should be chosen based on what fits and flatters YOUR body and feels authentically YOU!

Roz Kaur

PRO-AGE ACTIVIST AND STYLIST

STYLE ISN'T ABOUT TRENDS. It's about truth.

The best-dressed people I know aren't the ones constantly chasing what's new; they're the ones who know who they are and let their clothes reflect that. It's taken me years to arrive at a place where I dress for myself—with confidence, clarity and intention. But once I did? Everything changed.

I'VE SPENT three decades as a stylist, yet my own personal style has been the result of trial, error and, above all, time. When I was younger, I experimented with different aesthetics, trying on identities through clothing. Some worked, some didn't. But the one constant lesson is this: style isn't about getting it right; It's about refining what feels right for you.

EARLY ON, I fell into the trap of impulse buying. A trendy piece here, a "must-have" item there—only to realize those fleeting purchases never truly felt like me. Now, I invest in quality over quantity, choosing timeless brands that align with my aesthetic:

J.Crew for sharp essentials, Anthropologie for modern femininity, and Madewell for effortless cool. Now, my wardrobe serves me.

An investment doesn't always mean designer—it means thoughtfulness. It's about choosing pieces that last, not just for a season—like the perfect blazer, the well-tailored trousers, or the shoes that make you feel unstoppable. These are the building blocks of enduring personal style.

If there's one thing I've learned, it's this: style has nothing to do with age. And everything to do with confidence. There are no rules—and no age limits—on expression.

I LOVE a sharp blazer thrown over anything—it's a signature of mine that just works. I incorporate pieces of my Indian culture through jewelry, because it feels like a personal touch, a nod to my roots. These choices aren't dictated by trends, and they certainly aren't about fitting in. They're about owning my look—because when you dress for yourself, rather than for the approval of others, you carry yourself differently. Style isn't about perfection. It's about presence.

IF YOU'RE LOOKING to refine your own style—at any stage in life—start here:

- **Buy what truly excites you**. If you're unsure, leave it. If you can't stop thinking about it, it's worth considering.
- **Invest in pieces that tell your story**. Whether it's a well-tailored coat or a pair of vintage earrings, choose items that feel like you.
- **Lean into what you naturally gravitate toward**. If you love structure, embrace it. Prefer flowy silhouettes? Build around them.

- **Remember: signature style is an evolution, not a destination**. You're allowed to change, grow and refine—but always stay true to yourself.

Joyce Lee

CREATIVE DIRECTOR

GROWING UP, I was always fascinated by design. I didn't know what it would mean for my future, but I knew what caught my eye—a detail, a shape, a proportion that just felt right. I gravitated toward things that were well-made and well-constructed, even before I had the language for why I made those choices.

I REMEMBER WANTING a pair of glittery, translucent jelly shoes when I was young—like every other girl on the playground. My mom wouldn't buy them. She didn't like the idea of wrapping our feet in plastic. So, determined to have them anyway, I tried to make my own. I cut up plastic six-pack rings, taped them together with Scotch tape and slid them onto my feet. It didn't last long. But I was proud. I had created something.

IN MIDDLE SCHOOL, I fixated on Birkenstocks—the real kind, with the suede-wrapped footbed, molded sole and the two thick straps with just the right curve and buckle placement. They were $80, completely out of reach. But one day, while rummaging through the metal racks at our local Ross Dress for Less, I spotted a bright teal sandal. I kept walking. But then I paused—those buckles! Those straps. That sole. Real Birkenstocks—the Sydney upper, not the Arizona. They were my size. They weren't my color, but they were real. I bought silver paint at Michael's and transformed them to suit me. That moment taught me something foundational: fashion could be democratic, but it didn't have to be disposable. You could customize it, reinvent it, and own your style.

I think about that moment a lot—because it wasn't just about a shoe. It was about trusting my eye. Trusting that I could take something close and make it mine.

IN HIGH SCHOOL, I was voted "Most Likely to Become a Fashion Designer." My boyfriend at the time got "Most Likely to Be a Dancer on MTV's *The Grind*," which felt about right for the era. But while my classmates could already see that part of me, my parents had other ideas. Anything but something creative. Art school wasn't an option. Still, I had a practical side too, so I agreed to go to college—to study something "real."

I chose UC Davis and majored in Textiles and Marketing, telling myself I'd figure out the rest later. Only later did I realize I was already walking toward what I wanted—in my own round-about, determined way. I didn't think I knew who I was yet, but actually, I did.

AFTER GRADUATION, I moved to London to intern at *Wallpaper* magazine. On my first day, I found myself in their fashion closet surrounded by stacks of Louboutins, Manolos, Miu Miu... and Marc Jacobs. Glorious, playful, subversive Marc Jacobs. I fit into the size thirty-nine—a sign, maybe—and I remember thinking: I need to work for this man. I collected every magazine with even a peek behind the curtain of the brand. I wanted to be part of that world.

BACK IN SAN FRANCISCO, working at Levi's in denim R&D, I found an accessories design program at FIT. It was exactly what I needed—but another hurdle loomed: my mom still wasn't convinced. By then, though, I was quietly stubborn. This wasn't a phase. It was a calling. I applied, got in and moved to New York.

EVENTUALLY, I was hired to design bags for the Marc by Marc Jacobs diffusion line—playful, exaggerated proportions, chunky stitching and all the irreverent charm the brand was known for. Later, I moved into footwear for Marc Jacobs and Marc by Marc —and my childhood dreams collided with reality. I traveled to Italy to work with factories on lasts, heel shapes, leather selections. I had made it. But more importantly, I realized I had always known who I was.

Marc by Marc Jacobs represented that unapologetic middle ground I've always loved—bold but accessible, irreverent but thoughtful, nostalgic without being sentimental. It wasn't just a brand I worked for; it was an extension of the girl who customized her Birkenstocks and cut plastic rings into jelly shoes.

I'VE COME to realize that trusting your instincts—especially the ones you had before the world told you otherwise—is where true style and self-awareness begins. That younger version of you often knew exactly who you were becoming. We're all women who were once little girls, and she still knows the way.

Daryl K

FASHION DESIGNER

THERE ARE SO many options for dressing these days. I believe the body is made to move, and clothing should be designed with this in mind. Clothes that move with you come from both a thoughtful cut and fabrics that stretch. Fabrics woven with stretch, rather than just knitted fabrics, are more forgiving as they don't cling to curves. If you like fitted pants, look for fabrics with just enough stretch—too much can ruin the structure that flatters your shape. Curvy bodies benefit from flared cuts, which balance the line beautifully. In dresses and tops, the bias cut is genius: its fluidity allows for a sensual drape that defines the body elegantly and creates volume without bulk.

MOST WOMEN LOOK best in clothing that fits correctly—not oversized, not undersized. Conscious styling is the key to achieving personal style. Pair a fitted piece on top or bottom with a looser silhouette to define an area of the body, like the waist, shoulders, butt or ankles. A black or navy tailored jacket is a wonderful garment when you want to elevate your look with a sharp finish, and it can be paired with anything. Watch out when creating divisions on the body at the waist and ankles by pairing different colors, as this can shorten the line instead of elongating it. Simple looks are the most flattering—this applies to both silhouette and color choices.

YOUR CLOTHES SHOULD EXPRESS how you feel. Your day should be better because of what you wear. There's nothing worse than hating what you're wearing because it's uncomfortable, poorly fitted, or inauthentic—even at the office. Spend time figuring out a few looks before each new season to avoid stress when it's time to leave the house. This forethought offers the convenience that a suit-wearing man enjoys, never needing to consider what to wear on a busy workday morning! Shoes matter a lot: the right pair should go with most of your wardrobe, and comfort and style are equally important. Personally, I like dresses and skirts in warmer weather when legs can be left bare, and pants in cooler weather.

MANY WOMEN'S lives changed when they discovered a pair of my stretch leather pants—cool, practical, comfortable, sexy and versatile. The idea is to find an item of clothing that is your dream item, that is right for almost all occasions and that can be styled with anything. It's like a good friend in your closet.

DRESS FOR YOURSELF-YOUR body, your comfort, your mind, your mood.

Tiffany Wendel

STYLIST

THE TIME HAD COME. After thirty-five years in the fashion industry and collecting what I thought was my lifetime wardrobe of vintage, designer, and the perfect 501s from my dad, I had to face the facts. At fifty-one, my body changed overnight. My waist was thicker, my chest was bigger, and my jackets were tight across the shoulders. I stopped wearing the items in my closet because they were no longer easeful or comfortable. And as much as I loved looking at them, these pieces were also a constant reminder that I had outgrown them. They were no longer a great fit. After being the same size my whole life, I set my mind to cleansing my closet. I'd had "a really good run."

STILL, I love all of these pieces from my past that hold so many emotions because they are snapshots for me—memories of moments in time, of the joy I felt wearing them, experiences I had. I wasn't able to have nice pieces growing up, so each item is so appreciated and the story of getting it so exciting. This is my art that I collect: Vintage reworked flare Levi's from Jo Bush, from my days owning a boutique in L.A.; my favorite men's vintage trousers that had been my mainstay the past ten years; the BLK

DNM biker jacket I got for my fortieth birthday; my fringe jacket from Cheyenne. All items from L.A. circa 2000 that I still love. My pink velvet shirt from Barneys New York I splurged on back in the day, and the Dries pieces I picked up every sale season. Nobody told me my feet would grow with age?!? I am reluctantly passing on the Giuseppe Zanotti glitter boots I got on eBay, le sigghhhh, and my Chanel Dallas collection boots with spurs. It is time to let go.

My daughter, who is studying fashion design at Parsons, was born when many of these items were first in style, which means they are, thanks to the twenty-year cycle, just what she wants to wear. Seeing Lula in my pieces daily is both stinging and also fills my heart. When I see her wearing my clothes I resist blurting out "that was my favorite blouse I got in New York for fashion week" or "those were the jeans I thrifted in Idaho." Instead, I mentally tell myself the story of each piece, and I am in awe they ever fit.

WITH TWO THIRDS of my closet gone, it is now time to rebuild. But what does that look like, and when will my body settle in? I am trying new styles and am determined to have fun with it. I will prioritize keeping my confident sex appeal and rebuild with cool eclectic pieces that fit. Maybe I am now Diane Keaton, or maybe I'm Iris Apfel. It is all to be determined. I am going to let go and lean into rediscovery, and I take joy in seeing the next generation appreciating my pieces. Man, I rocked it—and with no rules. I am ready to continue the streak.

I CHALLENGE you to look at your wardrobe through this lens—what is comfortable, what is easeful and what feels good to you now? What I have realized is there is a power in letting go and an excitement in embracing this era. The new fashion project of experimenting and rediscovery is where it's at and I'm all in.

April Uchitel

CEO + FOUNDER, THE BOARD

GROWING UP IN SMALL-TOWN LONGMONT, Colorado, in the early '80s, the high school "ideal" was short, blonde and voluptuous. Teetering on five foot, ten inches, 36AA, with glowing red hair, I'd shrink myself in photos, wear sweats under my cheer uniform to hide my "toothpick legs," and zip into a massive red hoodie no matter how hard I'd worked on my daily outfit—just to hide inside.

This was the dawn of Esprit and MTV—Cyndi Lauper, the Go-Go's, Joan Jett, Blondie, Madonna—where color, accessories and makeup added a sense of both power and playfulness. They introduced me to the allure of individualism. This fun, rebellious style pushed against previous expectations and made me wonder if maybe I, too, was unique—and not a freak.

MY FIRST JOBS were in fashion. I drove thirty minutes, five days a week, to Boulder to work at Contempo Casuals, funneling every paycheck back into my closet: removable shoulder pads, cardigans with crest patches, bike shorts, Talking Heads-style blazers, parachute pants and bolo ties. We were encouraged to sell two-and-a-half items to each "guest" by adding two to three accessories at the register. And we needed to look the part.

From there, I managed Benetton on Pearl Street Mall in college—my high school sweats morphed into crazy patterned leggings worn under knit mini-skirts and sweater dresses. But outside the store, I felt like I was wearing a costume.

I MOVED to L.A. and got a full-time job in fashion. From Bridge to Contemporary, L.A. to New York, I wore the brands I worked for—but the clothes always felt like they were wearing me. My last stint was nine years at Diane von Furstenberg running global sales, where Diane herself once told me, "You look like crap in a wrap." Alas, she was not wrong—curves were required.

WHEN I LEFT fashion for tech in 2012, I was liberated by open floor plans, no dress codes, young creatives, and tech bros in jeans, sneakers, and hoodies. Yet I was still unsure of my style, having dressed the part for over two decades. Long past chasing seasonal trends, I craved a uniform. Slowly, I began to uncover my own style— shocked that it took me until my forties to do so.

I found myself most comfortable in a tomboy-menswear hybrid, leaning into vintage jeans, Nili Lotan army pants, men's button-ups and blazers, classic knits, striped T's, a dash of YSL leopard or Helmut Lang leather—and not a chiffon print or ruffle in sight.

After tech, I moved back to L.A. and into beauty. I'd started rocking a NARS red lip after DVF—it made me feel polished with little effort, a great counterpoint to my evolving "not trying too hard" wardrobe. I've worn glasses since ninth grade and spent years searching for the perfect frame. I finally found it in a Céline pair from Selima Optique—and when it was discontinued, Selima made me a 3D mold so I could have them forever. For over a decade now, those two signature elements have defined me—and I rarely leave home without them.

AT FIFTY-EIGHT, I'm the most confident I've ever been in my style. My boyish frame now feels like an asset; I know what flatters me and what image I want to project: cool, approachable, and confident. Fashion meets function. An urban uniform with a touch of playfulness—but never trendy. Birkenstocks and leather skirts, cutoff Levi's shorts, crossbody Clare V. bags, the perfect Buck Mason or Todd Snyder for Champion sweatshirt, a timeless J.Crew men's white linen button-down, thrifted blazers tossed over shoulders, pajama tops with boyfriend jeans and the nonchalant layering of stripes—making packing easy while eliminating decision fatigue. The DREAM!

IT TOOK me until my forties to uncover my style, and my fifties to own it. I've learned that confidence comes from discovering what works— and what feels authentically *you*—from truly knowing yourself, feeling at home in your own skin and letting the rest go.

Acknowledgments

This essay collection has been nearly thirty years in the making. The first essay was written when I was still figuring out who I was —and shaping this book through the decades has meant revisiting closets both literal and metaphorical, stepping back into styles, scenes and selves I've since outgrown. It has been a journey through memory and identity—one I could never have undertaken alone.

To the incredible Famous Last Words contributors—Sarah Clary, April Gargiulo, Joyce Lee, Stacy London, Daryl K, Roz Kaur, Nikki Kule, Meg Strachan, Megan Papay, April Uchitel, Tiffany Wendel, and Meg Younger—thank you for sharing stories that are vulnerable, heartfelt and rich with wisdom and style. I am honored.

Thank you to Anna David, who championed me for years before giving me the opportunity to publish this book and who, after reading my first sample chapter, declared, "You will never look at fashion the same way again." I am also deeply grateful to Zibby Owens, who published an excerpt of an early chapter years ago, offering the encouragement I needed to keep going.

To my editor, Monica Corcoran Harel, there are no words for how grateful I am—if there were, you'd make them sharper and funnier. Thank you for your insight, humor and joy throughout this process.

Thank you to my proofreader extraordinaire, Heather John Fogarty, and to book agent Kim Perel, whose guidance and creative insight were instrumental in shaping this book into what it has become.

Deborah Kirkwood, our bond over early Esprit fashion and a shared love for *The Official Preppy Handbook* has meant so much. Your patience in reading every word over the years, and your unwavering support, has been invaluable.

I am endlessly grateful to Audrey DiSpigna, who embraces a "more is more" philosophy in both fashion and friendship. Thank you for your encouragement, editorial guidance, and our long "wodcast" memos.

Rachele McGinty-Mock, I'm grateful for your limitless talent and for the way you see me so clearly. Thank you for translating the heart of this book into something visual, powerful and uniquely its own with your cover design.

To my family—thank you for supporting me as I became the person I strived to be. Your love, acceptance, and humor made it possible. James, Cameron and MacEwen, you are the loves of my life; making you proud means the world to me. Thank you for cheering me on through every draft, checking in on my writing during our daily carpool chats and reminding me to laugh along the way. Mom, thank you for being my confidant, for answering my call at every monumental moment in life and for giving me the freedom to explore, experiment and find my way.

To friends and colleagues—those I've known since the '70s and those I met along the way—thank you for inspiring and witnessing so many versions of me. For shopping sprees, fashion gambles, and endless conversations about who we wanted to become. You are all in these pages—sometimes incognito, sometimes called out—but always by my side and forever on the listening end of my enthusiastic (and very long) voice memos. And to Montauk, my loyal companion, who makes life better and never once complained about the long writing hours—there are so many walks in your future.

To my CrossFit coach, Ernest—thank you for always pushing me to find my strength and for standing by me as I sweated (and occasionally cried) my way to publication. And to Violet, who encouraged me decades ago to show up in the front row of her boxing classes, despite a diagnosis I feared would hold me back.

To the designers, artists, and cultural voices who defined the eras that shaped our world—thank you for showing the infinite possibilities of expression. From the fashion you created to the values you embody and the quotes I share within these pages, you have transformed my perspective—and now the reader's. In order of appearance: Ann Demeulemeester, Miuccia Prada, Carolina Herrera, Cynthia Rowley, Trina Turk, Mara Hoffman, Marc Jacobs, Diane von Furstenberg, Tory Burch, Jenna Lyons, Olympia Gayot, Isabel Marant, Ann Mashburn, Maria Cornejo, Karla Welch.

And finally, to you, the reader—thank you for opening your heart to these stories. I hope they awaken memories of who you once were, bring clarity to who you are today and inspire courage for the person you're still becoming.

About the Author

Christine Morrison is a renowned journalist and the creator of *writing in black and white,* a newsletter and online platform that explores fashion and beauty through the lens of aging. Every day, she challenges conventional narratives about growing older. Her work has appeared in *The Washington Post*, *The Boston Globe* and in campaigns for major fashion and beauty brands. A former Calvin Klein vice president and current member of THE BOARD, Morrison brings sharp insight and personal perspective to *Clothes Minded*, a collection of essays on style, identity and self-discovery.

Stay connected and read more at
writinginblackandwhite.com and
writinginblackandwhite.substack.com